WE DANCED!

A Devotional Filled with Excerpts …
From the Dance of a real Fairy-Tale ~~Romance~~
… Including Pract~~ical~~

LIN SONS

D1277813

Inspiring Voices
A Service of **Guideposts**

Inspiring Voices books may be ordered through booksellers or by contacting:

Inspiring Voices
1663 Liberty Drive
Bloomington, IN 47403
www.inspiringvoices.com
1 (866) 697-5313

ISBN: 978-1-4624-0811-5 (sc)
ISBN: 978-1-4624-0812-2 (e)

Library of Congress Control Number: 2013919834

Printed in the United States of America.

Inspiring Voices rev. date: 11/26/2013

Written for God's glory in honor of:

Buck who was my loving husband, partner in life, and best friend,

And

Bruce and Heather, our children, our life gifts of God's love

Marriage is not a ritual or an end.
It is a long, intricate, intimate dance together,
and nothing matters more
than your own sense of balance
and choice of partner.

—Amy Bloom

Contents

Introduction

Let's Dance—1-2-3-4

Love is like dancing. You can look at the steps on a paper chart. You can then place your feet on the floor into the paper footprints indicated. Take step 1, move on to step 2, then step 3, and finally step 4. You've accomplished the dance technically. What a concept! You can dance.

Not exactly! It takes lots and lots and *lots* of practice. You must do 1-2-3-4 over and over and over to be able to dance with a great deal of finesse.

Often when we marry, we believe we are in love and things couldn't get any better. Believe me, marriage takes constant work and refining, massaged with tender loving care. The final days you have together can be much more exciting and intensely more romantic than those early days of romance. Those early days are just the beginning.

This book, *We Danced,* is written to serve as a couple's devotional for God's glory. Whether used as a reading in the early morning or in the late evening, I challenge you as a couple to read an excerpt from our lives, think of your own similar but unique circumstances, and receive the dance tip as a tool to grow closer in your marriage relationship.

The Lord did a marvelous work in our lives. This is His story and for His glory!

He wants to do a marvelous work in your marriage relationship as well. Begin a new work to make your dance alive and vibrant from now till your last breath together. Continue to refine your marriage skills as you work toward the goal as partners through life. There are going to be times where you swing and your partner sways. There are going to be times when it might seem you are both fighting for the lead. At other times, you just melt into each other's arms and everything is totally synchronized. You two want that moment in time to last forever!

It's up to the two of you—both of you—to work to make those moments last. If you are willing to work, let's get started. Let me share excerpts from our dance to encourage the two of you!

Buck and Lin Step onto the Dance Floor

The scene opens with eight singles sitting around a table in a college cafeteria. Debbie, Donna, Carol, and I were attending a Campus Prologue Weekend sponsored by Millikin University in Decatur, Illinois for all high school seniors. While I had no intention of attending this university, I wanted to go with my girlfriends for the weekend. My plan was to attend another university but to use this weekend to determine my field of study. I planned to visit the colleges of music, education, and English to choose the degree I would pursue.

As with all love stories, my life began a wonderful adventure that November weekend. I began to learn what it meant to dance.

My friends and I were scheduled to meet a friend, Dave, who was then attending Millikin. He met us for lunch at the appointed time with three of his friends: Scott, Harold, and Buck. After a casual get-acquainted lunch, Buck invited all of us girls on a personally guided tour of the campus. Buck was quite the gentleman on the tour, opening the doors for us as we passed from one building to another. Like always, I took it for granted that I deserved that gentlemanly consideration. Later my friend pointed out (in front of Buck) that not once had I thanked Buck for opening the doors for us. From that moment on, my thank-you—with a curtsy at each door—became a highlight of the tour, and it was always accompanied with flirtatious laughter.

Slowly but surely, each of the girls dropped out of the tour. At the end of the tour, Buck asked if I would attend the dance on campus with him that night. I accepted his invitation, and we attended the dance in his dorm's recreation hall. We began talking—and we danced!

Somewhere in the process of the tour and the dance, Buck and I exchanged addresses and phone numbers. When I returned home, I wrote him a thank-you note for helping to make our Millikin University weekend memorable. Buck and I continued to correspond via written letters through the holidays.

Mid-January I received a letter from Buck. The letter included an invitation for me to attend a formal dance held at the Elks Club near the campus. I later found out this was *the* college dance of the year. I borrowed a blue-green brocade dress. We were to go dancing!

My heart pounded as I watched from my bedroom window as Buck's 1963 Olds pulled into our driveway. I waited upstairs but watched as he came to the door. He was very handsome and seemed quite relaxed and comfortable as he met my dad at the door. I made my entrance, and we talked with my brother and my parents.

We arrived at the hall, which was decorated beautifully in red and white for the Valentine's Day theme. The band played, and we danced only the slow dances.

At one point, Buck went to get some refreshments for us. When he brought the punch and offered it to me, it all spilled down the front of my borrowed dress. First impressions are often quite memorable in so many ways. We laughed together about our first formal dance and the sweet memory of the "oops" for years.

Those slow dances might best describe the beginning of our dating days. Letters flowed back and forth through the mail. There were few dates. His funds were low and he didn't have access to a car. In order to date me, he had to get a ride to his hometown eighty miles away, get his family car, and drive eighty miles in another direction just to pick me up for a date. Since I lived twenty miles from anywhere, he'd drive us to a theater, to a fair, to a dance, or to any fun event. Then, we'd drive back to my house ... and Buck would make the eighty-mile drive home. We were young, and it didn't seem to matter. It helped to keep our dating a privilege.

Dance Tip 1

It's easy to take things for granted and forget the word *privilege* in our vocabulary. For you as a couple, what was your greatest gift and privilege? Is there a sacrifice you two hold as a treasure from your dating days? Talk about that time together and think of those treasures of the past—and then your dreams of the future.

How can the two of you allow those dreams and treasures to spark a new meaning of the word *privilege* in your relationship today?

Excerpt 2

The Buck-and-Lin Dance Intensifies

As we slow-danced through the first six months toward that first kiss, I especially remember that though our dates were sporadic, every date was unique and different. Those dates included a car show in his college town, a dance, a movie, and skateboarding from the pavilion hill at a local hilly park down to the parking lot *in the dark*. I knew this guy was very interesting, that I would never be bored, and that life would be full of adventure and fun.

After our first year of dating, my family would invite Buck to spend the weekend so he didn't have the long drive for such a short time. Playing football outside with my brother (and throwing the football through the basement window) that first weekend made a great first impression on my parents! We played basketball often in the driveway—especially when Buck found out I didn't shoot a basketball "like a girl," but instead, with skill and accuracy. One of my first outstanding gifts from Buck was a basketball spray-painted blue, my favorite color.

My dad had a lot of respect for Buck. He was especially intrigued when Buck would come for a meal and share with Dad his engineering study of the week. Dad loved hearing Buck explain why tennis balls were furry on the outside, or why golf balls had indentions. That may have been fascinating guy stuff, but it left this girl yawning.

I remember the one and only time Dad read my letter from Buck. I was struggling with a life decision—whether to drink alcohol to fit in with the crowd at my high school or whether to leave it alone and not give in to peer pressure. In Buck's wisdom, he shared with me in that letter how he had faced the same pressure in high school and at college. His advice was to not let peer pressure dictate any of my life decisions. In many things I would have to take a stand, and this one decision would determine which path I would follow from there: giving in to peer pressure or standing on my convictions. That was *amazing* advice for a dad to read from the guy her daughter was dating.

Two years later, my dad was killed in a road construction accident when he fell from a piece of road equipment he was riding. The equipment ran over his chest and he died ten hours later. Buck drove us home from the hospital the night Dad died, and my world turned upside down. In my devastation, I had tried to be there for Mom for anything she needed; I tried to be the big sister to my eleven-year-old brother, Bob; I tried to hold down a new job; and I tried to make it in the world without my dad, who was my best friend.

After a few months, our dance of two years came to an abrupt exit from the dance floor. I told Buck I just could not handle all that life had dealt me and date him too. (Later I found out that Buck had planned to ask me to marry him that summer. I had *no* idea!)

We went our separate ways. I retreated to work and to my family. Lots of changes had taken place. After spending some time at the house and helping Mom get her affairs in order, she and I decided it would be best if I relocated closer to my work for the coming wintry weather in Illinois.

I found an apartment with my friend, Shannon, and I moved to within minutes from my work. Since Buck and I weren't dating, I didn't notify him of my move. I wasn't going to contact him. I'd been raised that it was the guy who was to pursue the girl. But, oh, how I was missing him! I wondered if I'd ever hear from him again. How would he find me? I dated a couple other guys, but it just wasn't the same. I wanted Buck. So I waited.

Finally, one day in the mailbox, I had a notification to pick up a package at the local post office. My girlfriend and I went for a drive that evening. On the drive I wondered who would send me something I had not ordered. When I opened the package, it was a box of stationery and a book of stamps with Buck's return address. That was it—no note, no letter, nothing—just a box of stationery and stamps. A couple of days later, I received a phone call from him asking me for a date. *Whew!*

The dance music began again.

Dance Tip 2

Our relationship began with dancing, followed by an exit from the dance floor, and then a return to the plan God chose for us. You see, He ordered our steps, just as He promises in His Word. He kept drawing us back for His glory.

Devastation comes in many forms. For Buck and me, it drew us closer eventually. We found strength in each other, and it made us stronger in our relationship.

While your circumstances may be quite different, how has devastation in your relationship turned you toward each other to focus together rather than apart?

"Misty"

The dance moves continued since Buck now had his own car. He'd moved to the University of Illinois campus to complete his studies toward his Bachelor of Science degree in Aeronautical and Astronautical Engineering. (B.S. of A.A.E.)

I had decided I was ready to date Buck exclusively. When I drove to the University of Illinois campus one Saturday night and told Buck that I only wanted him and no one else, his comment was, "We'll see!" We waited.

A few months later, there was another dance. My high school homecoming dance was approaching. I thought it would be a fun weekend to get dressed up and go dancing with Buck and many of our friends. Buck showed up that night with one red rose signifying his intense love for me.

I had envisioned this dance might be a reunion-type atmosphere with all my friends and classmates. As we danced in my high school gym, it was as though there was no one else around. In actuality, the dance turned out to be a time focused only on Buck, the only man in the world for me.

At some point while I stepped out for a moment, Buck slipped over and asked the band to play "Misty," our favorite dance song. As the music began, Buck reached out his hand to me in invitation to dance, and we danced. During our time on the dance floor, Buck told me he loved me, and in the middle of our slow, romantic love song, he asked me to marry him. I began jumping up and down saying, "Yes! Yes! Yes!" Our new adventure started as we began a new dance.

Dance Tip 3

God gives us special times to hold on to when the times get rough in our relationships. When life circumstances became challenging, Buck and I could play the song "Misty" and push them aside as we returned to that dance floor for a sweet remembrance.

What is the one thing that marks your dating time? Think of it as a "cornerstone" like Jesus is the cornerstone to us as believers.

What is the one thing you two would say was your foundation as a couple—your cornerstone?

Our Surprising Start!

Despite Mom's poor heart health, she and I were able to shop for my bridal gown and make wedding plans. Dad had always told me he could never give me away. It broke my heart that he couldn't be there to share in our joy at the wedding. Buck and I had a church wedding by candlelight. Those attending our ceremony were my brother, Bob, who was Buck's best man; Shannon, my maid of honor; Buck's parents; my mother; and a friend of hers.

As candles glowed, I entered the sanctuary to the rustle of the fabric of my dress. I took my place beside Buck at the altar in a forever moment in time. We repeated our vows, signed the papers, paid the minister, and began the dance as husband and wife. Our ceremony was followed by our celebration dinner with our wedding party at a restaurant in a nearby town—and we were off on our honeymoon.

Buck had accepted a job in St. Louis with McDonnell Douglas, and I was transferred to the St. Louis office of my company. We had three weeks to find an apartment, move, get settled into our new home, and begin our new lives as Mr. and Mrs. Buckley Sons. Those three weeks were rather eventful. We rented an apartment and rented the furniture to fill it. We loaded everything we owned into a five-foot-by-eight-foot U-Haul trailer (and had lots of space left over) and moved from Illinois to Missouri.

When we moved into our apartment, we were thrilled! We unpacked all our wedding gifts one morning. We decided I'd wash all the dishes and Buck would dry them. The sun shone through our window in the kitchen, and we were laughing and talking. When I pulled the plug at the bottom of the kitchen sink to let the water out, all the water came out onto our feet and the kitchen floor. We immediately opened the cabinet doors under the sink and discovered there were *no* pipes! What a messy surprise, but oh, so much fun!

Our next adventure after we got the apartment in shape was to locate where we were going to work. We had passed McDonnell Douglas on our way into St. Louis, so now we needed to find the office where I would work.

For some reason that day, we decided to drive two cars. Buck was leading in his car and I followed in mine.

That's when the accident happened. We had gotten off the highway at my exit. Since Buck was leading, I was looking intently at the building numbers to try to find my new office. Little did I know there was a stop sign in the middle of the block due to a side street on the left! Suddenly I saw Buck's car stop and heard the crunching of metal from my car ramming his! Neither of us was hurt; it just hurt Buck's pride and caused me embarrassment.

You see, as Buck assessed my car and tried to make it work, he pried the fan blades out away from my radiator. That prying left holes in my radiator. It made perfect sense, but it didn't work. The accident was a lesson learned on both our parts, and it was a very expensive memory.

Our jobs as engineer and secretary taught us a lot. We have memories of apartment walls that were too hot to touch when we'd return from a weekend summer trip. We had been given plastic curtains that were actually two pieces of plastic (one was the liner) that blew and crinkled in the breeze. We had an oven that would hold only one pan at a time. We froze in the winter when the apartment furnace quit working. We piled every single blanket and comforter we owned on top of us to keep warm, and that layer of "comfort" was so heavy we could hardly move underneath it. After the first year when our lease ended, we moved and a new chapter began.

Dance Tip 4

God's Word tells us that when we are weak, He provides our strength. (I Cor. 4:10) Whether your strength came from crunched metal in a wreck or bending blades of the radiator fan, where have you two found your strength? Talk about it. Open eyes lead to open hearts.

When did an "oops" in your relationship on both of your parts determine your strength as a couple?

Scampering in the Ozarks

Buck and I went on our first camping vacation in the Ozarks, a favorite spot of his family as he was growing up. We rented a tent camper to pull behind our car and headed out on our adventure. We set up the camper, went to the store for food, and started the grill. *So* good! As we walked around the campground, Buck recalled the spots he and his family had fished, boated, and vacationed near the dam. I had never been camping so all of this was totally new to me. I eagerly followed his lead since I had not been to this part of the country and wanted to learn about my new husband.

The first night we camped, we learned that the greatest asset to camping was a level trailer. Our necks and shoulders ached the next morning, but we looked at those aches as part of the adventure. We were having a fun vacation. The temperature was perfect and there was no rain. *Sweet!*

The second day was filled with hiking, sightseeing, and me watching Buck fish. We cooked our breakfast and dinner meals, and all was going quite well till …

We settled into the tent camper for the night. Just as we were into a really deep sleep, something landed on the top of our camper with a huge thud, waking both of us with a start. We immediately got up, dressed, packed the camper, and moved to the nearest Holiday Inn for the remainder of our vacation. Whether the thud was from an animal native to that area (which we couldn't find in the dark), or just some kids from the campground playing a practical joke, we decided a Holiday Inn was more to our liking for privacy and safety.

Dance Tip 5

We often think we're in control of our relationship and circumstances. Just then, life turns upside down and a new adventure turns out even better than we'd planned. God says that in everything we are to be thankful. We exhibit that thankfulness in our marriages by being a more effective witness for Him.

When did a change of plans upset all of your plans but work out best in the end? Have the changes in plans taught you two to be more flexible? Did those changes allow you to grow closer together on this adventure of "marriage," or did they become a wedge between the two of you?

Celebrate Your Differences

Y ou've heard the expression, "opposites attract." In the relationship between my husband and myself, the extent of that term was almost an extreme understatement.

We were *so* different. We soon realized we could either allow those differences to become an asset in our marriage, or those differences could become a wedge used to drive us apart little by little over the years. I guarantee this celebration did not come immediately for us in this dance of marriage. It was a learned process.

Allow me to use an illustration. Buck and I had been invited to visit some relatives in Indianapolis, Indiana. Our driving trip from St. Louis to Indy was quite pleasurable. We enjoyed driving and often used that time to plan our activities, set future goals, or to just be silly. It didn't matter. We loved being together—it was a part of the dance.

On this particular trip, as an example, we wanted to discuss the step to become parents and plan the timing of our family. It was fun to talk about what an addition of a little person would mean and the changes that our child would necessitate in the near and distant future. It was fun to guess what he or she might look like as well as what distinctive traits from each of us the baby would inherit.

Everything was going just dreamy till we hit the outskirts of Indianapolis, and my husband handed me the map. We were eager to see our friends and explore this unfamiliar city. While driving, he located their address and found it on the map. *No problem.* I found the street—even the cross street—and was so proud to have established that.

However, since they were located in the middle of the city, all those straight crossing lines on the paper just looked like a bowl of spaghetti to me. I realized I was in a very uncomfortable place, and I was embarrassed. I couldn't make any sense of that mess, but my pride would not allow me to admit it. Buck needed my help at that moment, and I couldn't do what he needed.

We had quite a heated discussion in the car like, "Turn here, no, that wasn't right. It's a dead end." "Okay, let's see, if I turn the page in the direction we're heading, maybe that will help. After all, how can I find where we are if N is straight up and down, and we're going east, which is to the right? So, if I turn the page so that east is up, then maybe that will help. Right?"

It didn't. We were lost and completely turned around. We had to stop and let Buck get his bearing. I was in awe as I watched Buck logically make sense of that spaghetti mess and get us going in the right direction.

It took both of us, and our own unique abilities, to negotiate this path called marriage. We each had brought very special, unique, and quite different gifts to our marriage. Early on, we each tended to see our own gifts as superior to the one who didn't have that particular gift. In this instance, I most definitely did not have map-reading skills.

However, my gift was unique. I had a tremendous sense of direction. If we went to a place one time, I could get back to the place exactly as we had traveled there the first time. And without a map, I could also get us back to that same location from any direction in that area. Buck couldn't do that. He *always* needed a map. Because of his analytical engineering mind, if he had a map, he could go anywhere (with me in tow).

When Buck asked directions to a place we'd been a number of times, I could not understand his lack of directional ability when he was so smart in other areas. This was a big-deal difference between us to the point of "World War III" type of discussions, complete with *heat*!

After years of dealing with this phenomenon, and the Lord's help to refine the celebration of our differences, He taught us that each gift could work together in different sets of circumstances for our good as a couple. Amazing!

Dance Tip 6

God does not condemn us just because we don't match someone else. He created us to be unique, different, and set aside for His service.

What are the major differences between you two as a couple? Have you learned to celebrate those differences and to see them as part of a complete picture? Are you allowing each individual the freedom to express his or her strength for the betterment of your marriage? Do you, instead, allow the uniqueness of the individual to become a voice for commendation, comparison, or condemnation?

How does your marriage celebrate and edify each other's differences to be used for His glory?

EXCERPT 7

New Dance Steps Take Shape

O ur second year led to new dance steps. We decided to try our moves toward parenthood. From my morning sickness to equipping a nursery to welcoming our new son, Bruce, complicated with my mother's stroke, life became overloaded once again. Our dance steps changed from high anticipation to tears and to pride and joy in our new son and our connection to the future. We danced!

Our dance soon was defined by moving playpens, car seats, formula, and diapers as we traveled from St. Louis to Mom's home three hours away every weekend to care for her. We even bought a new home in the country. Lots of shuffling and two-stepping around obstacles allowed us to settle in as a family unit. We made memories over the next few years that included our quarter-acre garden, getting to know families in our neighborhood, and establishing lifelong friendships.

It was Buck's idea to invite my mother to move in with us when her funds were depleted for her private care needed due to her stroke. That presented additional challenges as we welcomed her into a totally foreign environment. Bruce provided entertainment and a wonderful sense of delight and fun. He lightened her heavy heart due to the condition brought on by her stroke. Trading times between our house and spending time back in what was familiar with my brother and his family over the next year and a half, we all decided Mom would be happier back in Illinois where she would be close to her friends and family in her own environment. She was grateful to be with us, but lonely for her "familiar."

The move was great in that she was in an assisted-living environment where she enjoyed creative activities and shared recipes from her days as a cook. She could also enjoy more convenient visits with family and friends. We honored her by visiting often and sharing our hopes and dreams with her.

On our last visit, Buck and I went out to dinner with Mom; my brother, Bob; and his wife. We told her we were expecting our second baby, hopefully a little girl, since we already had our boy. She was delighted for all of us. Bob and his wife were expecting six months ahead of us, so she'd be a double grandma in the coming year.

However, that joy quickly turned to grief as a second stroke claimed her life a few days later. More challenges meant new steps to learn.

Dance Tip 7

Often we are stretched beyond all limits as we progress through this process in life. God tells us to go forth and multiply, to train the children up in the way they should go, etc. As for in-laws, life circumstances such as health, age, or living conditions draw our strength beyond what we ever could have anticipated.

How have children and in-laws impacted your relationship as a married couple? As you seek the Lord to provide the elusive strength in all these circumstances, how is He rewarding you two? What will you take away from these special times as nuggets to plant in your garden of growth?

Buck and Lin March to the Beat of a Different Drummer

L ife picked up to a steady, prevalent beat of a march as Buck's career demands increased. He was required to attend classes to improve his work contribution in the new computer programs. He taught classes the other nights of the week to further his team skills. We became involved in church and school activities as well as YMCA Indian Guides and Indian Princesses, Boy Scouts, and church choir. This time in our lives was so busy! We were constantly shuffling schedules so that at least one parent was home with the children when life circumstances demanded the other parent was not. Rather than dancing close on the dance floor, we began drifting apart to individual marching steps as we stared at and admired each other across the room.

However, we prided ourselves on our togetherness, and we shared common interests rather than separating or drifting apart physically like many of our friends chose to do. In comparison to them, we were doing very well. Just because we had little -- if any -- time left over for each other, we were committed to love each other no matter what. We began to settle for less than the best in our marriage and accepted this time as a phase entitled, "it will be better later." "Better" wasn't coming anytime soon.

As a strike at Buck's work demanded he work alternating shifts from first to third to second to third to first with no time to even think about couple or family activities, the stress began to take its toll. We knew things had become too much when slammed doors became the norm. I delighted in running the vacuum while Buck was trying to rest. Dishes clanked and pots and pans rumbled to a disturbing rhythm rather than that flow we had enjoyed the night we danced to "Misty" only a few years before. We needed help, but both of us were too nice to address the issues in fear we might have major upsets. I believe we thought if we ignored these problems, they would disappear.

Buck and I had married for life and were committed to make our marriage the forever kind of love. We'd not only committed to each other, but to God. Buck told me on the way to St. Louis on our honeymoon that he wanted our marriage to be one never-ending date. How were we going to keep that dream alive when disillusionment marched so deeply through our relationship?

Dance Tip 8

The onset of disillusionment often creeps very slowly into a relationship. For us, the challenge of Buck's career demands and our activities with church, school, and community all were good things. But we had trouble finding balance.

Ask the Lord to provide insight for both of you to assess the necessary changes in your schedules to make your couple time the top priority. He will help in this area if you invite Him into the equation. He provides just the right dance steps.

How about you two as a couple? Is this an area that needs work? Are you willing to ask for His lead?

Read on.

EXCERPT 9

God Took Our Hands and Led Us When We Had No Strength

When we were at our lowest, God showed His faithfulness to meet our every need. At our church, we were invited to attend a meeting for couples. We were encouraged to attend a marriage ministry weekend that seemed worthwhile. We needed something!

One of the couples that presented the information was from Buck's college choir. They shared how this weekend ministry had helped their marriage. As a couples group, we decided to attend this weekend to focus on our couple communication. Buck used to tell everyone he agreed to attend just to get Lin's problems fixed. Once that happened, everything would get back in line. He really believed this! He packed his favorite book to read, his swim trunks to enjoy the hotel pool, and we were off to a weekend of "fun."

We attended the weekend full of wonder. What could it possibly hold for us? Four couples from across the United States presented the weekend communication material. It was amazing to hear their stories and how much their stories paralleled ours. We could see they had found something we lacked (obviously), since they were teaching and we were such eager students.

The key for Buck and me was the talk on Saturday night—that the Lord not only wants to be Lord of our individual lives, but He also desires to be Lord of our marriage as well. We had never heard that before, but it made so much sense! As we returned to our motel room that night, Buck and I knelt before the Lord and confessed we had not reflected Him to each other. We asked His forgiveness and invited Him to be Lord of our marriage. We renewed ourselves before Him and began to receive the love He wanted for us as individuals and as a couple. That began a renewed dance of our lives together. No issue would ever become more important than our love for each other in Him.

At the end of the weekend, not only had our eyes and mouths dropped wide open by the truth of God's love and His Word to us, God called us to His service as a speaker team for the marriage and family ministry.

When we returned home, we made an announcement to our children, Bruce and Heather, who were eight and four: from that time on, Jesus would be heading up the Sons' household. We had no idea where the new adventure would take us, but we knew we were His for whatever, whenever, and wherever He wanted us.

Dance Tip 9

What does *lordship* mean to you as a couple? *Lordship* often takes on the meaning of demand and control if we look at it through the eyeglasses the world provides. As we look at lordship through God's eyes, we see a definition in the form of servant—love, kindness, putting the needs of others before our own. Jesus laid down His life for us.

God may not be calling you to full-time ministry, but He does call us to full-time love, service, and devotion to each other.

Are we as individuals willing to lay down our lives for Him? Are we as a couple willing to lay down our lives for each other in Him?

EXCERPT 10

Then There Was the Hole!

B
uck, Bruce, and I moved from apartment living to our first house in the country outside of St. Charles, Missouri. When the new house construction was completed, we moved into our home in the fall. It was too late to have any sod down till spring. Yes, our yard was mud for six months.

Bruce was three and displayed his independence in playing in the yard alone without me. He used his "tools" and made racetracks for his trucks and cars. He also learned to fly kites. He just *loved* playing outdoors.

He came in one day and informed me he wanted to dig. So I gave him some spoons, a spatula, and a small shovel he had as part of an old gardening set. He announced he was going to dig a deep hole, a *big* hole! Of course, I cheered him on, thinking to myself the attention span of a three-year-old wasn't too long and he would tire of this project once he realized that Missouri clay was hard like cement.

Bruce started by loading spoonful by spoonful of dirt onto his dump truck. When the truck was full of dirt, Bruce pushed it to another location and dumped it. Over the next few weeks, we began to note our young son's drive and determination. The hole that started with a few spoonfuls of dirt eventually became a hole five feet wide and deep enough to hide our three-year-old son. What a man!

Dance Tip 10

Determination and perseverance are wonderful traits. In fact, I believe they are gifts from God and used to instill within us a new strength we need to march on our walk of faith. Life often hands us challenges spoonful by spoonful. It's what we do with the small challenges that determine how we handle the monster challenges of life.

God used the traits of our young son to strengthen us. How are the traits of your children building and growing you two to celebrate your dance as a couple?

EXCERPT 11

Strawberry Hives

That little baby I was expecting before Mom died became the little girl we'd hoped for. We named her "Heather." As a little girl, our Heather loved strawberries. I planted several strawberry plants in a small patch behind our garage. Heather and I watched those plants grow, produce white blooms, then green buds. We waited eagerly for the day those buds would become fresh red berries.

Slowly the white blooms withered, giving way to lime green buds—much too slowly for a three-year-old who was experiencing the berry-making process for the first time. We checked every day, and a little time later those green berries had become white and much larger.

Heather's eyes were full of wonder as she continued to anticipate eating those juicy red sweet strawberries. I encouraged her to leave the berries till they were fully red and ripe. She watched over the next few days and exhibited a great amount of patience till she just couldn't wait any longer. As several of the berries ripened, Heather picked and ate them.

Within the next few days, she came in from playing with the announcement she itched and didn't feel well. When she changed clothes, she had lemon-sized welts all over her body. She was allergic to the strawberries and had developed an intense case of hives. (Writing this makes me itch as I remember how miserable she became as a result of giving in to temptation!)

Dance Tip 11

Temptation comes in all forms. Those forms may take the shape of sports, exercise, job, hobbies, food, alcohol, sex, etc. We face temptation in some form most days. It is what we do with temptation that determines our growth in the walk of faith. When we resist it and wait for the very best, we are rewarded. When we give in to temptation, we suffer the consequences of our actions.

How do you handle those things that tempt you? How does it affect your relationship with those around you, especially your mate?

Our Huge Quarter-Acre Garden

When we decided to purchase our first home in the country, we happened upon a place that was a half-acre lot. Immediately I saw the possibility of a huge vegetable garden. We moved, got settled in with Bruce, and had no lawn until spring—but we had our first home.

We asked the local farmer to plow our garden and get it ready for planting. Then we began to plant—which Buck had never done. We planted green beans, corn, potatoes, tomatoes, squash, green peppers, peas, onions, and cucumbers.

We also planted three apple trees along the north side of the garden. As we tended the garden, we had an immense amount of food. We were able to give away grocery bags full of food to the neighbors and still had enough food to can for ourselves for the upcoming winter.

Buck and I laughed as we worked. I teased him about his crooked rows. He pointed out we could get more in each one if they were crooked than if they were straight. Bruce and Heather helped snap the green beans, shell the peas, and shuck the corn. That garden proved to be one of our best family projects and just a dose of how God readily blessed our meager efforts with His abundance.

Dance Tip 12

The seeds that take root in early marriage must be maintained to fruitfulness. If those seeds have been constructive and have manifested positive fruit in your lives, you have a harvest of blessing.

If there are seeds that have taken root that have become destructive, it's time for a weeding to keep those invaders from destroying your marriage from the inside out. The enemy comes in. It's up to us to work together to take a stand for a plentiful harvest for His glory.

What are you building within your garden of a marriage?

EXCERPT 13

Our Perfect Truck

S oon after we moved to the country in Missouri, Buck decided to buy a truck. We wanted to plant trees and do some landscaping, and get a lawn mower. Besides all of that, he told me every man needs a truck.

We watched the classifieds, visited a few dealers, and waited for the perfect truck. Buck came in from work one day with the announcement he'd found his perfect truck. He bought it, and the man would deliver the truck on Saturday to our home.

Saturday was a big day of anticipation and excitement for Buck. After a few hours, the green 1948 Ford pickup rolled into our driveway, followed by the owner's family in a car. When the gentleman got out of the truck, he was three feet tall. Buck introduced us, and we had a great visit with him and his family. While I knew we were getting the perfect truck delivered that Saturday, Buck had left out the part that he had purchased the truck from a little person. He told me he just wanted to see how surprised I'd be and how I would handle this unique and most unusual anticipated event of the arrival of our perfect truck.

Dance Tip 13

God's love comes in all sizes and shapes. We must maintain open hearts to those around us who share and spread His love as we all rejoice in Him. Perfection is not determined by how everything fits into our mold. Perfection is achieved only when it fits into God's mold.

How many blessings has God bestowed upon you that have come within surprise packaging?

EXCERPT 14

The Two-Step to Humility

I remember a real wake-up call one weekend that Buck and I presented a marriage communications weekend as a couple. In fact, I believe it was our rookie weekend. While the details and specifics are a little sketchy, I remember Buck was amazing. He remained calm and retained his humility in the Lord. He seemed to lead and guide as a real man of God.

I was so "Martha-like" that I got lost in the details. (See Luke 10: 38-41) My focus was more on how we did, if we did everything right, etc. I truly was so humbled at the privilege to present and to be used to speak to married couples that I just didn't want to do anything wrong. Notice the focus on "I." I was still stuck in the performance trap. But one comment from that weekend stayed with me through all our years of ministry. Our mentor commented that I loved being up there speaking. I humbly replied, "It's not about me."

However, though I believed that statement to be true at the time, I realized my focus wasn't truly on the Lord and on what He could do. I *did* love the speaking and being a leader. I *did* love leading others and listening to the "*oooo's* and *ahhh's*" when it was over. That was until the time I really saw with my own eyes what the Lord would and could do in the lives of others. It had absolutely nothing to do with how something was done, whether the weekend details were included or omitted. It was all about *Him*, and had *nothing* to do with us.

I learned a very sobering lesson in humility that weekend that transformed my life and heart for the Lord and what He could do. Buck saw and knew that truth in his spirit early on. It took me a little while longer to learn this part of our dance.

Dance Tip 14

Even though God chose two women to illustrate His point, men also sometimes fall victim to "busyness" rather than having a "servant heart." Have either of you determined to be a Martha when God might have needed you to be a Mary? How is the Lord opening your eyes to serve Him with an attitude of "it's not about me" versus "it's *all* about Him"? Bowing in surrender and dying to self is always followed by a moment or two of humility.

Are you two singing His song and dancing to His master plan?

We Began the Foxtrot

In addition to our communications weekend and our call to ministry, Buck had taken classes at his company in a new program in engineering. That program allowed more efficiency in using the computer in design and drafting. Buck was confident this would open new doors for his career.

Buck was informed that Piper Aircraft in Vero Beach, Florida, was his company's first customer to use this new program. Buck had not only learned and applied this new program to his present engineering career, he had taken additional classes and became an instructor. He requested an application from Piper, filled it out, and left it on top of his dresser, waiting on the Lord's timing to submit it. Our wait took one full year.

When Buck finally sensed it was time to submit his application to Piper, our adventure took off on "greased rails." Buck and I went to Florida for his interview weekend. The interview that was supposed to take a couple of hours took five! Their comment was that they had no idea they needed someone of Buck's qualifications until his résumé landed on their desk.

We had prayed for God's confirmation. The confirmation came when Buck told his company back in Missouri of his offer and plans for our move to Florida. His company offered Buck a different job, his "dream job" with the company, even though Buck had asked God not to give him a choice. Not only did they offer him his "dream job" plus more money, they gave him the opportunity to see what he would be doing in wind tunnel testing using this specialized computer program. God made it abundantly clear that Buck would not like the job because of unrealistic demands despite the increase in money. We were on our way to Florida!

Dance Tip 15

"Greased rails" only happens when your will and His will are in alignment. Alignment does not come from perfection. It comes when we surrender all of who we are to His will, not our own selfish ways and desires.

What would "greased rails" look like in your relationship to take you to the next step of obedience to His will? Enjoy the ride!

No Funds—New Home

While we could see God's affirmation of our move to Florida, we did not know the area where we might live. We looked around for housing and found a house in a town outside of Vero. There were better schools for our children and lower taxes. The owners required $30,000 down in the original discussion. Since we had not sold our house back in Missouri, we turned down the property.

The owners phoned us the next morning and invited us back to their property that night to talk about the house. We thanked them but told them there was nothing to talk about since we had no funds. They insisted we make a return visit!

When we arrived, they told us they had worked out a deal they thought would work well for both of our families. They had papers placed on the table. Their plan for us was to rent their house till our house in Missouri sold. They told us they had been praying for a Christian family to move in and take ownership of this house. They believed we were that family. When we looked at the contract, it was just as they said. However, the numbers had changed. Instead of $30,000 down when our Missouri house sold, they had changed the number to $3,000. God's provision and plan were put into action.

We made a wonderful home there, a true lighthouse in that community. Since we were located at the beginning of the subdivision, our friends would stop by after work for a Pepsi, some tea, or just to talk. Our band director and his wife would come by for a chat after school, and many would come by for prayer or a need.

A minister and his wife lived across the street, and they were often a source of encouragement for us. Attending their small church enhanced our family's vision for God's call to missions via marriage and family ministry. Their ministry to us began with a container of chili the first day we moved in. They invited us to attend their mission conference. We heard a new and unique side of Christianity. We learned God could use real people as His vessels to bring the world to Him through Jesus Christ. From South Africa to Jamaica to Haiti to international missions organizations around the world, we heard the need to pray for His workers as they shared Christ with others. The small congregation of forty-two people had a *big vision* and huge hearts for God's work that helped to increase our perspective of sharing the gospel.

We had moved to our house in November. That meant Christmas was just around the corner. In a strange new place, knowing no one very well was a big challenge for our family. We missed the familiar—friends and family, and something that resembled normal. With all of that, I remember sitting with Buck under our Christmas tree, crying as we listened to our ministry group from home sing love songs and Christian choruses to us on tape. However, in our sadness and homesickness, we were reminded that the Lord had sent us to Florida for His purposes, and we would rejoice.

We remembered a saying, though not necessarily scriptural: "When God gives you lemons, make lemonade." Our lemon at that time felt like Florida, so we made our lemonade on Christmas morning. We opened our Christmas gifts, packed a picnic lunch, and headed to the beach. We laughed and played and made great memories with Bruce and Heather. We determined to enjoy God's creation, which helped changed our attitude from sadness to gratefulness for our new adventure in Him!

Dance Tip 16

Obedience brings sacrifice. Sacrifice may not involve a cross-country move. It may not be a change in climate. It may be only an attitude adjustment. Guaranteed, it will mean using lemons to make lemonade!

How is the Lord asking the next dance step of obedience for you two as a couple?

Open the Door!

Those words ended a day of tears and turmoil in my life, and I will hear those words echo forever. The Lord blessed our family that day. I will forever give Him praise.

Prior to those words, things looked a little grim around the Sons' household. We had moved to Florida only a month earlier, which meant that we had been settled in only a couple of weeks when our friends (a family of four) from St. Louis called to say they would be spending the week between Christmas and New Year's with us. Additional friends, also from St. Louis, phoned with their plans to be on vacation in Florida, and they also wanted to spend New Year's Eve with us.

Before I knew it, we were having company. I had spent our last few dollars on groceries, tracking every penny, recipe to recipe, to buy only what I would need and nothing more. How would I be able to stretch the groceries I'd just bought so that I could feed six more people—in addition to our family of four—for a period of about ten days? (And this was just the beginning. We found our home often became a very popular vacation spot once we moved to Florida. ☺)

I cried to the Lord and asked, "How much are you expecting of us?" With the extra guests to feed for such a lengthy time, what were we going to do? The Lord would provide because we had no more resources. We would have to trust His provision.

My friend had sent me a special music tape with a song on it that served as encouragement to me during our move. The words of the song were taken from Luke 6:38 which reads as follows,

> "Give, and it shall be given unto you; good measure, pressed down, shaken together, and running over, shall men give into your bosom. For with the same measure that ye mete withal it shall be measured to you again." KJV

We were just sporadic in our giving up to the point I had heard that song, but somehow those words became life. Those words were a spiritual principle, a cycle God had put into place for us to use. We had our eyes opened to what true giving meant, and we have continually been amazed to watch this principle become alive in our walk with the Lord.

We also had read this in Malachi 3:10.

> Bring ye all the tithes into the storehouse, that they may be meat in mind house, and prove me now herewith, said the Lord of hosts, if I will not open you the windows of heaven, and pour you out a blessing, that there shall not be room enough to receive it. (KJV)

While I believe all of that was true, and we were being faithful in this new area of our Christian walk, I really didn't see what it had to do with this particular situation of guests coming and no extra funds for entertaining. I had discussed with my friend that we were having tough times financially with the moving expenses, that we were having guests, etc., but because of my pride, I could never share with her (at least at that point in my life) how desperate things really were. I just told her I was looking to the Lord to provide and trusting Him because there was absolutely nothing I could do.

This was the day, three days before our guests were to arrive, and I was sitting at our dining table, praying and thanking the Lord for whatever it was He needed to teach us at that time. I then went over my recipes one more time to see what I could do to make a difference. Just then I heard the voice of a man coming up our driveway yelling, "Open the door … open the door!"

As I looked out my window and rushed to the door, I saw our UPS man carrying a very heavy box. He hurriedly dropped it in my kitchen, said it was meat, asked me to sign the form, and he left after wishing me a Merry Christmas. Of course, my curiosity was stirred, so I opened the package. I found a twenty-pound turkey, a twenty-pound beef roast, and two New York strip steaks, but no name or note. I immediately phoned my husband to tell him of our mystery package, and we were both ecstatic. God's Word had come alive—and I will ever praise Him for His provision. He was our "Jehovah-jireh," our Provider.

Later that evening, my friend phoned to see if her package had arrived. I cried and said, "Yes!" Since she was a single mother and had just gone through a divorce, I knew she didn't have this kind of money. I scolded her for doing such an extravagant thing. Her comment followed: "But Lin, the Lord sent that gift. I didn't do anything. My boss gave me a $2,000 bonus for Christmas, and I have more than I need and some to give away. It's all His anyway. He impressed me to send this for your family at this time. Enjoy!"

It was only then I could admit to her how desperate our financial situation was, and I asked her for prayers through this trying time. I thanked her for her obedience to the Lord and for her love and blessing in our lives. Together we prayed and thanked the Lord for our connection in Him.

Those words "open the door!" were the Lord's way to "open the windows of heaven and pour you out a blessing, that there shall not be room enough to receive it." He knows and provides our every need!

Dance Tip 17

In my anguish, I saw the impossible. With His eyes, the Lord saw the possible. Listen to His voice; follow His lead; walk in His path of blessing. Dance before Him as you explore what He has for you!

How is the Lord "opening the door" to meet your most pressing need?

Swing-and-Sway Sacrificial Giving

I remember when we were living in our Florida house and had not yet sold our house back in Missouri. We were stretched financially to the max, couldn't make our credit card payments, and had only enough to make our house payment.

All of a sudden, God put a couple in our path at our church. They could not pay their apartment rent. He'd gotten hurt and could not work. They were fishing and crabbing at the inlet to put a meal on the table.

Guess what! The Lord taught us a new swing and sway. In obedience to the Lord's direction, we gave our rent money to the church so this couple would have a place to live. We had not done anything like this ever before, because He'd never asked us to give all that we had for Him.

When He directs and leads, we have two choices: obey or look out for our own selfish needs. We chose to obey.

We were amazed at His provision to pay our rent, pay our payments, and to know His sense of a job well done because of our obedience. It didn't make any logical sense, but His ways are not our ways.

Dance Tip 18

Would I recommend giving the only money you have away always? *I absolutely would not*, unless He leads through His Spirit. However, when He directs, obedience is recommended. You obey; He gets the glory. You have an incredible testimony because you get to know Him in a deeper way and much more intimately.

You two can dance before Him in His joy! We danced!

The Word ... Alive!

But my God shall supply all your needs according to his riches
in glory by Christ Jesus. (Philippians 4:19 KJV)

As I stated, serving in ministry often brought many challenges.
The job changes, moves across the country, and living on faith
when there was "more month than money" became a regular way
of life for us.

One summer in June, we were once again having guests to our new
home in Florida. Three families were visiting our home within a very
short period of time. Two couples came for dinner only, but they were
on vacation and traveling to other parts of the state. However, one family
visited with their four children for an extended ten-day vacation. A few
days before their visit, after the bills were paid, our family had seventy
dollars to buy food for the two-week period until Buck's next paycheck.
I prayed before we went to the store that God would stretch that seventy
dollars as far as He could to feed this family of six plus our family of four
for ten days.

As you might imagine, by the end of the visit (with no money from
them except one picnic lunch at the beach), my cupboards were becoming
bare. I prayed and asked the Lord for His creativity to make our last time
together as enjoyable as possible.

The lady guest in our home had been up during the night with their
two-year-old and had decided to sleep in. (I'd never understand how she
could block out the noise of the other eight people in our small home—
everyone was excited.) Everyone wanted to spend every second of this
vacation together. My husband had to work during the day, while our
children, Bruce and Heather, had enjoyed entertaining their childhood
friends at the beach or at home playing board games, watching TV, or
fishing at one of our local twin lakes.

What a week it had been! The evenings had been spent going for walks, playing at a nearby park, working on marriage ministry talks, or just relaxing. We parents had actually allowed all the children, ages six to thirteen, with the baby already asleep, to babysit themselves while we went for a cup of coffee at a local restaurant. While nerves had become a little frayed with ten people stuffed into our small home for ten days, none of us wanted the vacation time to come to an end. Since they lived 1,300 miles away in the St. Louis area, we all treasured each moment.

I did the last bit of their laundry before they left, took orders for breakfast, and talked with the family about the last day's activities. Our guest directed a question to the kids: "What has been the most fun while visiting the Sons?" Of course, the girls said very emphatically, "Going to the beach. We have to go at least one more day to touch up our tan. Please, may we go to the beach?"

Our guest's youngest son requested one more fishing trip to the local dock. He wanted to go fishing one last time. The two older boys and his dad were not excited about that idea since they had already been fishing there and had come home empty-handed. However, the five-year-old insisted. We really didn't have any other plans, so the guys were going to fish one last time together. With bait and poles in hand, the van was loaded and off they went on their fishing expedition. We girls would go to the beach to catch just a few more rays.

There was peace and quiet in the house for a few moments … until I looked in our freezer and realized there was no meat for the evening meal. I had no money to buy extra anything. I had spent all that I could afford to spend to feed all of us. Though they had bought picnic supplies one day for a trip to the beach, I had been able to stretch all the other meals with no problem. However, tonight was a celebration dinner and I had no meat. As I closed the freezer door, I prayed silently, *"Lord, You know our needs. Thank you for providing for us, in Jesus' name, Amen."*

I thought to myself, *"If I have to, I have plenty of vegetables. I can sauté this, and casserole that, and fix a salad, etc., and meat really won't be missed. But it's up to You, Lord."* I deliberately didn't mention the lack of meat to our guests, mostly out of pride. I just didn't want to dampen our day or to even sound like I might be hinting they buy meat. The Lord was our sufficiency—not our friends.

We girls put on our bathing suits, put lotion on the baby, and packed a picnic lunch, and we were off to the beach. Dinner was a problem I would deal with later.

The baby laughed and laughed as the white foam from the waves rushed to shore to tickle his feet. Our girls had become even better friends during their time together, and they were eager to talk and walk on the beach. Then they would run to the ocean and get knocked down by the waves after they got over the "ditch" of deep water close to the shore. It was an absolutely perfect day and fun to get away from it all and relax. My friend and I had some time to reflect on the week, on what the Lord was doing in each of our lives, to give Him praise for the good and the bad, and just to catch up with news of all our friends of thirteen years we had left behind in St. Louis.

We girls arrived back at the house first, so while the girls showered, I started meal preparations. I began peeling and chopping vegetables while my friend put the baby down for a nap, and the girls later went for a walk. The guys pulled in a few minutes later, and they had a *catch*! The five-year-old was so excited. He knocked at my kitchen door, and through the glass window I could see he had something in his hand. When I opened the door, he screeched, "We caught some fish! Where can we clean them?" Our friend wanted to show the boys how to clean fish, so I gave them a cutting board, a couple of pans, and a couple of knives. I was not concerned with how many fish they had caught. I was just happy the time had been great and everyone seemed happy.

When all the fish were cleaned and brought to me to place in the refrigerator, the little guy asked if we could eat them tonight for dinner. I said, "Of course, since you caught them and you're leaving tomorrow, we'll have a special fish fry tonight." His face absolutely beamed. I figured it was the least I could do on their last day here, right?

When I counted, I found God had supplied the fish on that fishing trip—one fish each for dinner that night. That's right—ten fish for ten people—a real celebration of God's faithfulness to supply all our needs from His riches in glory! (Philippians 4:19 reminds us: "But my God shall supply all your need according to his riches in glory by Christ Jesus.")

When my husband said grace at our meal that evening, I wanted to scream and shout—and inwardly I did in my heart. Outwardly, I just whispered an extra special "Thank You." When we trust Jesus as Savior, follow Him as Lord, and take hold of His promises, we can count on His provision because He knows our every need, and He supplies "according to His riches in glory."

That couple was a presenting team in ministry alongside us. We chose not to share our story about how God had supplied through those fish till a year later on their next visit. What a testimony we all have because of one little five-year-old guy who insisted on one last fishing trip, and because of a big God who provided above all that we could think or ask!

Dance Tip 19

There's just something about fish. Jesus used fish to provide a meal in the Bible. This story is found in Matthew 14: 15-21.

He used fish in a modern-day tale of turning the impossible to the possible as only He can do. Our hearts danced before Him for His provision in His joy!

Gone fishing lately?

EXCERPT 20

The Anonymous Christmas

We met all kinds of people in our travels. One family was so great. The husband had crushed his ankle on his job, had gone through several surgeries, and was told it would take at least a year for his ankle to heal properly. The wife cleaned houses to help feed their family of three small children. That's tough at Christmas when Dad can't work to make the money for the bills, let alone the extras like Christmas presents.

What an opportunity! Our family could be a blessing! The key was how to do it anonymously! The anticipation of that secret built up within our family as we shopped and gathered gifts, wrapped them with love, and prayed for the Lord to show us how we could do this delivery without getting caught.

We placed all the gifts in a couple of big bags and delivered them on their doorstep before the sun came up on Christmas morning. We could only imagine the looks on the faces of the parents as well as those children's faces as they discovered their gifts from the Lord to their family for a very special Christmas memory.

The only question we could come up with was, "Who had the greatest Jesus joy?" Was it those who received the gifts anonymously? *OR*, was it the ones who secretly shopped and wrapped and delivered them?

Dance Tip 20

Part of dying to self allows us the privilege of serving others. Ask Him what gifts the two of you have to use in the lives of others. Pray and then discuss how He might lead you to stand in the gap for another couple or family.

How has the Lord made the two of you aware of opportunities to serve anonymously?

His Love Is Sharing

One of our unique situations in living in Florida was meeting a gentleman and his wife at a local Bible study. This gentleman could not work due to a brain injury as a young man. He loved the Lord and seemed to connect with Buck and me as we consistently attended the study. Sometimes he would call Buck just for prayer due to health or family concerns. Other times, he'd walk about five miles to our house just to sit and talk with the two of us.

The last time we saw this man was the day he came walking up the driveway. We sensed there was trouble. When we went to greet him, he was devastated and in tears. His wife had left with their children. He didn't know what to do or where to go. He was totally distraught and had walked to our house to ask for prayer for her, for the kids, and for his next steps in the Lord. He was confused and had no other place to turn.

We invited him in, prayed together, and asked for God to order his steps, for wisdom as to what to do next, and for the privilege of this man to see the Lord's work at every turn. After having some iced tea together, we gave him a bag full of fruit and snacks, and he was on his way.

We've not heard from our friend again and don't know where the Lord's adventure took him. We trusted him to the Lord's care and continued to pray for His care and provision for our friend in the Lord.

Dance Tip 21

Love through sharing time is often the greatest gift we can give to others. Jesus spent time with those who needed Him. He's always willing to spend time with us; He's never too busy. When we come before Him, His focus is on us. We don't deserve it, but we receive His time and focus and love as very real gifts.

Spend some time in reaching out to others who need His love. It does wonders to improve the finesse of your dance.

Are you willing to be His representative in the lives of those around you?

Our Very Special Christmas Gift

Our move to Florida was followed by the privilege of my husband working four weeks and only getting paid for two in order to keep the job. (Notice the tongue-in-cheek tone of that last sentence.) It was a challenge for us in our faith walk described earlier in our dance. But in the midst of the money challenges, we had some great times!

When Christmas came that first year in Florida, we had set aside a certain amount for Christmas gifts—a total of forty dollars for our family's Christmas. The kids each had ten dollars and we had twenty dollars. They did their shopping and we did ours. We eagerly waited to see how much fun this Christmas was going to be!

On Christmas morning, we opened our bedroom door. We found a series of large paper footprints on the floor, leading from our bedroom out to the living room. We all opened our gifts, had breakfast, and observed a big package placed against the wall. It was marked for Dad and Mom. Our children told us that box did not contain the present. It was only the box for the real thing. They opened our front door. Wrapped in paper and with bows in the shape of a heart was a porch swing for Buck and me.

The kids had pooled their money, bought the swing, and stored it in the outside shed. After we had gone to bed on Christmas Eve, Heather had stood watch outside our bedroom door while Bruce climbed out his bedroom window, assembled the swing, hung it, and placed bows in the shape of a heart on it. They had then laid out the paper footprints to lead us to the best Christmas gift of their love!

Dance Tip 22

The Christmas gift that year was never the item contained within the package. The most precious gift was that two young children used their time, talent, and treasure creatively to consider the needs of others. They were being "Jesus" to those who needed a touch of His love.

We have many opportunities to use our time, talent, and treasure to meet the needs of others. How might we apply their "gift" in our lives as an example?

Four for Two

Our dance really became more of a side step when the holidays were over. After Buck was employed at the Florida company, and we were all settled in for a couple of months, the company offered its employees "such a deal." In order to have a job, workers would work four weeks during the month and get paid for only two.

Yes, we danced around in near panic as we wondered how we could possibly live on half salary for an indefinite period of time. We had two houses now, with a mortgage on one, plus rent on the other, plus credit card debt after the move. "Overwhelmed" seemed like an understatement!

However, we trusted that the Lord had a plan including these circumstances, so we trusted He would provide. We could not see any reasonable way that could happen. We knew God is a God of the impossible and, though our faith was stretched beyond all things reasonable, we were still together … and dancing.

I remember one night after months of this challenge. Buck walked in and I was exhausted from bill paying, debt collection calls, and more month than money. I didn't say a word of complaint. He just saw the table with the bills spread out. He put his arm around me and thanked me for handling it all and doing such a great job with the bills. Buck said he'd take over our finances from that time on.

I appreciated his sensitivity to what had become an insurmountable task for me. Some forms of dance, such as ballet, often take the form of only one person dancing. However, marriage is a two-person dance. We needed to "dance" in the midst of our circumstance, and this time, it took two to dance.

At that moment, his hug and love secured him one more time as my real-life hero.

Dance Tip 23

I understood at that moment why God calls the female the weaker vessel. I had all the clerical skills plus the personality to deal with the phone calls. But I needed a hug and someone to just say, "I've got it." God knew I couldn't handle this load. He sent along just the right dance partner.

The greatest joy is giving our love away to the one who never asks. Try to increase your awareness of your partner's need before the need is mentioned. Step up to meet that need, and then watch your partner dance before the Lord!

How have you two looked beyond the moment and circumstance to determine the need of the other?

Excerpt 24

No Compromise

As we approached one of the communication weekends we were to lead for the ministry in Florida, the organization tried to convince us to "pad" the cost to the attendees by adding a ten-dollar addition to the weekend charge. In doing so, we could begin to build up a "kitty" for any unexpected ministry expenses, etc.

As Buck and I prayed about that scenario, we decided to take a firm stand. We thanked them for their suggestion but decided to stay with only the true actual cost. That way, we would not compromise our faith in the Lord to provide. We would not pad the fees "just in case" the Lord didn't provide.

During the next weekend event, the Lord met our needs as a ministry. We needed exactly $1,420 to meet the monetary needs of the weekend.

During a presentation, the couples were told of our exact need of $1,420 to cover the weekend expenses of motel, meals, printing of materials, gas for our guest speakers, etc. They were then given plain white envelopes and asked to pray about giving a gift to offset those expenses. Later we would collect the envelopes, and whether they were led to give a gift or not, we needed each couple to turn in a sealed envelope. They were asked not to place their names on them. Each gift was to remain anonymous.

After the weekend had ended, during our leadership team prayer and praise meeting, we opened all of the envelopes. When we added up the cash plus the checks that had been included in the envelopes, the total was exactly $1,420! We bowed in a humble prayer, thanking the Lord for His provision and for honoring our "no compromise" stand.

Dance Tip 24

God tells us in His Word that He will give us what we need for the day. A bird goes hunting for food every day, and every day the bird finds enough for its need. If we are able to trust God to feed the birds, we need to trust Him to meet our every need.

As in prior stories in this book, Buck and I were living proof that God meets every need if we submit that need to Him and wait.

How are you two being challenged in this area of faith today?

Did I Hear You Right?

During a period of "more month than money," we had very little money to buy groceries for our family. Rather than buy for the whole week, I bought only enough groceries for the weekend on my Friday shopping trip. In addition to buying at the grocery store, there was a farm truck parked alongside the road selling huge bags of potatoes for three dollars, so I bought one of those bags as well. I thanked the Lord for His provision and proceeded toward our home.

On my way, as I was passing another grocery store, the Lord impressed me to pull into that grocery store parking lot, park the car, and buy groceries for a family of five who were friends of ours. I knew it was a rough time financially for them as well, but I did not know any of the specifics of their money situation. My question to the Lord was, "Did I hear you right?"

I pulled into the parking lot, but I must say I was in a desperate quandary. I began a conversation with the Lord. "Okay, Lord, I'll do what you say. I just left my grocery store, and that store's prices are cheaper than this one. Do you want me to turn around and go back there?" The answer was "no." I needed to shop at this store. I continued my conversation with the Lord. "But I only have twenty-five dollars left for this week's groceries. That's every dime I have. I'll give it up for this family, but I have no idea what this family needs. Since this is *your* idea, you're going to have to show me exactly what to buy. (Notice the sassiness amid the surrender?) I have no idea what they might need. Please show me what to buy … and thank you for doing this."

I entered the store with no idea of what to place in my shopping cart. As I walked up and down each aisle, it was as if I "knew" what to choose and what not to choose. For instance, I bought a chicken, but nothing to go along with it. I bought a head of cabbage, but no meat or anything that would make a meal. I bought eggs, but no bacon or ham or sausage. I bought paper towels, but no toilet paper. I bought one box of cereal, but no milk. I also purchased a few other items, but none of the items went together nor made any sense if I were planning meals for a week for a family of five. When I checked out, the bill came to $22.90. *Amazing!*

I stopped by my house to put my groceries away and then quickly proceeded to my friend's house. I knocked on the door with two bags of groceries in hand, and an additional two bags plus a bag of potatoes in my car. My friend was shocked, and asked what I was doing there with all of this food. I explained that the Lord had impressed me to buy groceries for their family, and I was simply following orders. I also explained that none of the combination of items would make a meal, but I knew the Lord directed me to buy these specific items.

She wiped her tears and invited me inside. (I didn't ask about the tears. We women just get weepy sometimes.) I showed her what I had purchased. I again explained none of this made any sense, but I was eager to see what the Lord was doing. We began unpacking the bags.

I bought a chicken. She had a package of noodles and a package of stuffing in her pantry, but needed a chicken to go with it to make the meal. Not only would she have two meals for her family from this, she would also have chicken salad sandwiches for lunches for her three children.

I bought a head of cabbage. She went to the freezer, opened it, and pulled out a huge package wrapped in aluminum foil. Her mother had sent her home with a big piece of corned beef, and now she could make her husband's favorite meal: corned beef and cabbage. There would be plenty left over for a meal or two after their feast.

I had bought eggs. She had bacon. The eggs and bacon, when combined with the potatoes I shared with her, would make another evening meal. She would make that meal one night and use the leftovers in a casserole for an evening meal later in the week.

She hugged me, and we cried and prayed together. We thanked the Lord for how He knew just what was needed for this family, and how He provided through one very confused, bewildered but obedient messenger.

As we rejoiced, my friend shared with me that while I had been shopping, she had paid all their bills, and had only ten dollars left to buy groceries for the coming week. While I was shopping, she was praying and crying because she just could not see how she could make that ten dollars stretch to feed her family of five for the following week. Now they would be able to eat heartily. We would all give praise to a God who loves us and wants to show His love in the most extraordinary way.

As I drove away from her house that day, my heart danced all the way home at the goodness of our Lord.

Dance Tip 25

God says His ways are not our ways. He disciplines us and rallies us to do His will. It's all about Him! It's not about us. He knew exactly what this family needed. He just needed a willing vessel to supply those needs. That way, all of us could grow and give a wonderful testimony to the glory of our King!

Celebrate His glory today. Listen when you hear a command, and answer with a "Did I hear you right?" totally surrendered as His willing vessel.

EXCERPT 26

Quilt for the Homeless Man

I was new to quilting and had decided to cover a worn quilt with a new quilt top. I cut up pieces of old fabric, pieced together a top, made the backing, and *voila*! With a little time and a few dollars, there was a new quilt to keep in the car for a beach blanket or to snuggle under when the moist Florida air turned chilly and the kids were cold.

On one particular Wednesday evening at the end of our church service, a transient traveling down US 1 on that cold Florida night stopped by our church to ask for a place to stay out of the cold. The church turned him down, even though our building had a room that had only one entrance from the outside and no entrance from that room to the rest of the building.

Buck and I were very upset that the church turned this man away without providing him a warm place to stay. As we left the parking lot, we prayed as to how the Lord might use us to share God's love with this man. We drove out of the parking lot. On our way home, we knew we could give away our quilt to this man if we could find him.

We turned around and went back to town, going up and down US 1 and looking in all the nooks and shadows for that homeless man. Finally about a mile from the church, we saw him on the sidewalk of a strip mall.

Buck approached him with the quilt under his arm and told him we were at the church when he asked for a place to stay out of the cold. We wanted him to know we didn't agree with the church, and that we wanted him to have the quilt to keep warm. At first, he would not accept it. However, as Buck shared how God had laid it on our hearts to try to find him, he could see our sincerity and accepted our gift of God's love.

Dance Tip 26

God took our scraps, pieced them together, and turned them into a blessing for someone who needed warmth and God's love. Our lives often look like those scraps. In the case of Buck and Lin, we were two people from opposite areas with different talents and abilities, who were placed together to be a blessing to others by using the materials we had pieced together for His glory. We must let the Master shape us and connect us in the exact right way to reflect His beauty.

Is He asking you to take your scraps, piece them together, and become a blessing to proclaim His name to someone who needs His love?

EXCERPT 27

Our Ministry Begins

Never forgetting the reason we were called and moved to Florida in the first place, Buck and I contacted churches about our ministry. We talked with our new friends and acquaintances about the importance of God's Word in our marriage.

Over our first year in Florida, we waited on God's timing to tell us when to launch the ministry, specifically when and where to contact motels, etc. During one Sunday morning church service, Buck and I looked at each other in the middle of the service and *knew* it was time. After contacting our local paper and having them do an interview with the family, Buck and I scheduled our first ministry weekend in the state of Florida.

Twelve couples attended. Buck and I wore all the hats of servants that weekend. We registered the couples. We established contacts and a contract with the local motel. We served as a speaker team, teaching throughout the weekend. We later switched from speaker team during the last talk of the weekend to the reception couple as we opened the sliding doors in the presentation room to a wonderful wedding reception complete with cake, punch, nuts, and mints. Even though we had no ministry community to share in these various jobs, we wanted to make that weekend so very special for those couples. What a joy to serve and to love those couples!

It was an amazing privilege to see what God had put together in Buck and Lin as a couple serving together. What I lacked in organization and meticulous detail, Buck supplied. When Buck was not as bubbly and outgoing in people skills, I supplied those. What I forgot, he remembered. Oftentimes, when I hadn't even thought of items to pack or the location of our talks, Buck had already taken care of it. At the end of that first Florida marriage ministry weekend, we stood with thankful hearts and absolute awe at God's provision as we worked as a team to begin our ministry in a new state.

Dance Tip 27

We are incomplete. No one has it all. As a couple, begin to focus your thinking on how a lack in one is found as strength in the other. Then begin to celebrate that you are not alike, nor are you perfect, but together you can be made complete as you seek that completeness, not in each other, but in Him.

It's a time to rejoice and dance (Colossians 2:10).

Promoting the Ministry in Palm Bay, Florida

Buck and I had been sent by the Lord, via a new job for Buck, to open the state of Florida for this marriage ministry, as was mentioned earlier. One of our dances was to promote the ministry among local churches.

I had attended a ministerial association meeting in Palm Bay to explain the marriage ministry to six local pastors. Out of the six, one pastor talked with me after the meeting and set a date for the presentation to his church. Later, Buck and I met to develop and print brochures to share with other congregations in the area a month in advance of our presentation event. We were very appreciative of this pastor's enthusiasm to get God's Word to the community families.

On the night of our scheduled event, we showed up at the church in plenty of time to set up, meet with the pastor, and prepare to greet the couples of the community. When we pulled into the church parking lot, it was full to the brim, with cars everywhere! We were so very excited and encouraged as we unloaded the car with the projector, our notebooks, the slide cases, and handout materials. We were eager to meet all the couples that wanted to make a difference and influence those around them. We were amazed at the number of cars in the parking lot.

As we entered the sanctuary, the pastor approached us. We shared our excitement with him and began our set-up process. He told us that all the cars in the parking lot were there for a Boy Scout banquet held that night. We were disappointed, of course, but went ahead and set up for our presentation as directed by the pastor. He had been diligent to publicize our event to the community, and he hoped some of the couples could come to our presentation.

We waited and waited and waited for an hour … and no one showed up. At the end of the hour, Buck and I packed up everything and left the church very disappointed. We asked the Lord if this was just a test and what we were to learn from this ordeal. He impressed upon us that He sent us, we were faithful to go, and that was all that He needed from us. He'd do the rest. It wasn't about us. It was about Him!

We danced to His music and followed His lead.

Dance Tip 28

Oftentimes, we are called out to go on a journey for one purpose. However, during that journey, we find He had an entirely different plan in mind. When that happens, do not be discouraged. Rejoice and seek Him as He leads and guides. Keep on dancing before Him!

Buck's One and Only Birthday Party

Buck had never had a real birthday party, so I decided to plan one for him. What fun the kids and I had as we planned the party! I phoned our friends from two churches as well as from the neighborhood to come for a Sunday afternoon party after church.

As the cars started pulling into the carport and people started arriving to wish him a happy birthday, he was more than just a little surprised as we ate and shared in our potluck meal celebration.

When we finished, I gathered everyone together in the living room and asked him or her to share one thing they recognized that made Buck special to them. Many shared their thoughts and memories, which were very uplifting and encouraging to Buck. One sharing came from a dear friend who recognized Buck for his consistency. He said he could always count on Buck. Buck never waivered or compromised his morals, his actions, or his walk of faith in the Lord. The day was such a blessing and a complete surprise to the man who walked humbly before the Lord—my husband.

Dance Tip 29

Between us privately, I always teased Buck about being stuck in a rut. However, his consistency was the balance for my impulsiveness. Together, we had the best of both worlds. My spontaneity added the spark, and his consistency was the flywheel as we danced throughout the path of our life together.

How do your special qualities provide balance with each other? It's a great discussion over dinner on a date.

Two Left Feet

As a married couple, did you ever have a time when nothing went right between you two? When a comment was made, and it was construed as criticism? When an action took place, and it was assumed it was rejection? When you got dressed, and the outfit you'd chosen wasn't pleasing to your mate, and their "helpful suggestion" became an unpalatable offense? When you drove the car, and you didn't do it right; you either went too fast or too slow? When you chose the restaurant, and your mate voiced an alternative or at least an objection to the dining experience?

At one point, we had months of that type of dance in our relationship. While I admit the negatives often came from me, neither one of us could find one happy, pleasant, or positive thing about the other. In fact, I'm certain my husband wanted to open the door and throw his hat in as a test before entering (and perhaps he even wondered why he'd chosen to enter at all).

Neither of us could point a finger toward one action or comment that had gotten us out of step. There wasn't one thing that had caused this major stumbling across the dance floor where we stepped on each other's toes as we maneuvered through this awkwardness. We were uncomfortable in each other's presence. We couldn't agree on anything without receiving contradiction from the other.

The only thing we did agree on was that no matter what, we both wanted our marriage more than we wanted our own way. We were determined that these major flaws or hurdles between the two of us were not of the Lord. We were not going to allow them to defeat us in being His representatives to the world around us. We did know this time that each of us dancing with two left feet was from Satan.

We knew the Lord was our source of peace and joy. We determined to come together before Him, admit where we were in our relationship, and ask Him to help us through His Holy Spirit. We had run out of energy and enthusiasm. We needed more help than either of us could muster. We needed to place our marriage once again in His hands to make it through this chaos. We also knew we could not continue like this and maintain a positive home life for our children.

Together we agreed to go to the Lord in prayer. We bowed and prayed and waited for Him to restore our joy and love and hope in His strength … and we waited.

As we waited over the next few days and weeks, He began to redirect our steps on His path instead of our own. He set our feet on His solid rock foundation of our faith in Jesus Christ who had called us out as His own.

In those moments of answered prayer, we realized we were just like every other married couple. We were weak when we tried to be married in our own strength. Our marriage was fragile and needed the glue only the Lord is able to provide. We were vulnerable to *self*ishness if we did not focus on dying to self and placing our mate's needs above our own. We had learned early in our marriage that *joy* comes from putting J - *Jesus* first, O - *others* second, and Y - *yourself* last. We both had stepped into "self," and that was a most uncomfortable mess.

What had started out and maintained a syncopated rhythm in harmony had within minutes turned to being out of step, marking time to a strained melody of discord. We needed the Lord to guide our steps, to set them on His path, and to take our two left feet and give them order, purpose, and direction.

He provided it all. He was and is to be praised and honored for untangling our troubled mess and continuing our steps in His service as His dance team of Buck and Lin.

Dance Tip 30

"Self" leads to *self*ishness that leads to discord. Discord leads to disunity and the battle begins. In our case, "self" had to be removed. "Self" needed to be replaced by the strength that only comes from the Lord.

Yes, we were just like every other couple that ran out of ourselves. "Two left feet" described that time in our lives. We just could *not* get it together in our own strength. When we were humble enough to bow and ask for His help, He was sufficient to supply our need.

How is this concept applied to your relationship?

EXCERPT 31

Bible Teaching *Explodes!*

When we led Bible studies in our home, often people did not understand when we talked about a personal relationship with Jesus. How could we eternally trust Him in everything? At one point, a friend came to me in an almost challenging mode. She insinuated I had a special "in" with God because He spoke to me through His Word as we faced various circumstances. I assured her that He wanted to speak with her personally as well and that He would do that if she began to rely on the Holy Spirit for His counsel and leading as the Word promises He will. She left quite skeptical, but I hugged her and encouraged her to stay on her knees before the Lord and address whatever issue was bothering her heart.

A couple of weeks later, I had a knock on the carport door, and as soon as I opened it, she burst through the door announcing that I was no better than she was. The Lord had spoken to her, and they had made the connection that I had told her was possible. She was eager to relate her story.

After our visit where we spoke about having a personal relationship with the Lord, for several weeks she had laid out every detail of her past before the Lord and sincerely asked through His Spirit for His comfort. He assured her that she was His child, and He met her in His love. In her prayer time through tears, she was led to the passage in Isaiah 54:4.

> Fear not; for thou shalt not be ashamed: neither be thou confounded; for thou shalt not be put to shame: for thou shalt forget the shame of thy youth, and shalt not remember the reproach of thy widowhood any more. (KJV)

She requested I read these words, but the meaning escaped me even though it had obviously provided incredible relief and comfort to her. She related the following story from her life.

She had been a widow at a very early age with young children to feed and clothe. With no skills or training for any type of job, she had prostituted herself in order to put food on the table for her children. Later she had come to know the Lord as Savior and had married and had more children. But her past had long hung over her head. She just couldn't get free from it.

On this day through the Bible—God's personal "love letter" to her—she received His peace. She knew on that day she was loved and forgiven for the first time ever in her life, and she left our home a *free* woman, no longer in bondage to the past sins of her widowhood. To Him I give all the glory and honor and praise to watch a heart set free!

Dance Tip 31

God does not hold our past over our heads. We choose to do that all by ourselves. We are condemned only because we are the ones who condemn. God is not capable of condemnation (Romans 8:1–2). He took on all sin, including ours. John 8:32 states, "We are free indeed."

In what ways do you need to find release and freedom in Jesus Christ for a heart set free?

The Bed Collapses!

O ne of Buck's pet peeves was our old antique bed. My grandfather had won our bedroom set for my mom's wedding gift by working a crossword puzzle in the local newspaper. It was *old*! The mattress and springs were held up on wooden slats that fit onto wooden rails of the two sideboards—most of the time. Occasionally the sideboards would spread just enough to allow the slats to fall down to the floor. This happened twice after one of our moves, when the movers hadn't aligned the boards correctly to fit on the rails.

You guessed it! One night, just when we had gotten fully relaxed and deep into sleep, Buck turned over, the slats gave way, and his side of the bed fell to the ground. I'd never seen Buck move so fast as he did when that happened. I truly think that was one of the few times I saw him really, really angry.

After the second collapse a couple of weeks later, Buck went to work devising a method of wires crossed in an X to give stability, complete with turnbuckles to adjust the tension. That was a most effective engineering approach to the problem. Each time we moved to a new location after that, Buck would specifically take this contraption and turnbuckles with us in our car to assure that the movers would not put our bed together. His design worked marvelously and ended the middle-of-the-night episodes that were absolutely hilarious—if you weren't the one awakened by falling to the floor due to the bed malfunction.

Dance Tip 32

Engineering ability and expertise combined with antique treasure became a marvelous combination through the years. Pet peeve turned sweet memory. How has a similar vexation turned into true joy in your marriage?

The Palmetto Bug Hits the Fan!

After a long day at work, Buck came home exhausted and really looked forward to a good meal, a relaxing evening with the kids, and a good night's sleep. We had a meal. Buck helped Bruce and Heather with a couple of homework questions. Then we went for a bike ride and watched some TV.

We then settled in for a good night's rest. At 2:00 a.m., all of a sudden Buck jumped up out of the bed and turned on the light. I was startled to say the least and asked what the problem was. He was shaking each of the covers, almost hitting the ceiling fan, like he was looking for something. He explained a palmetto bug had hit him in the middle of the forehead. We realized the bug had flown across the room, gotten caught in the swirling air of the fan blade, and been knocked onto our bed, hitting at just the right angle to land in the middle of Buck's forehead!

We searched the covers, sheets, and bedspread for the critter. We found it and Buck flushed it down the commode. He absolutely hated that part of God's creation—as in *could not stand them*—so to be attacked in the middle of the night by one hitting him in the forehead was indeed a most traumatic experience.

Dance Tip 33

What was God's purpose in that incident? Who knows! It made for a good laugh over the years, but it was certainly not funny at the time. God created all things, for which we are most thankful, but not all of His creatures are welcomed ... especially as an interruption to a good night's rest.

EXCERPT 34

Heart "Palpitations" in a Country Club Setting

B uck and I were invited to a Christmas dinner party at the Vero Beach Country Club sponsored by his employer at the time. We had made arrangements for our special evening out.

We entered the country club and visited with several friends. Buck introduced me to several new acquaintances as we went through the buffet line. The room was lit by candlelight and the setting was lovely. There was the social discomfort that happens at most office events. We didn't drink and didn't know very many people, but we smiled, minded our social graces, and enjoyed being together once more as we danced after the club cleared the dance floor for the celebration enjoyment.

At the end of the evening, Buck noticed that his heart was racing once again. (Earlier in the afternoon prior to our leaving for the club, Buck had come home from working at the church trimming bushes, trees, grass, etc. He stretched out on the floor to rest and noticed his heart was racing very rapidly—up to one hundred beats per minute. He felt fine; there was no pain, just an irregular heartbeat. We got ready for the club and thought a relaxing evening might help his heart to settle down.)

We drove home and went to bed, hoping for a restful night's sleep. At 5:30 a.m., Buck awakened me to the fact that we needed to go to ER due to the continued racing heartbeat. I immediately phoned our pastor and his wife to inform them, and I asked if we could stop to pray together before going to the hospital. We prayed that the Lord would undertake Buck's care as the Great Physician.

Upon arriving at the hospital, his heart continued to race as the ER staff monitored him. However, within fifteen minutes as the doctor was checking Buck's heart, it kicked over to normal rhythm (and after that, it continued beating regularly for the rest of his life). We thanked the Lord for answered prayer and praised Him once more for His goodness. After further testing with a heart specialist, we found an irregular heartbeat is fairly normal. In fact, the doctor had experienced this condition often throughout his own life.

That Christmas dance at the country club became more precious as we realized the gift we had been given. We were truly able to celebrate the life we had been given to teach and tell others about Jesus Christ and what He had done for us for His glory.

Dance Tip 34

Most couples have experienced a life-changing event. Discuss how that event or events put your relationship with each other and with the Lord into a whole new light.

How has that event changed your perspective as a couple? Do you value life more preciously? Do you focus on "life" instead of perfection, pretention, or performance?

Bruce and Heather's First Drives

B ruce had promised Heather the first ride with him after he got his driver's license. After Bruce drove us home from passing his driver's test, I got out of the car and Heather got into the passenger seat and off they drove to Dairy Queen.

My heart was in my throat as my two "babies" were both leaving the safety we parents had been able to provide. Now they entered the world of adventure and uncertainty. Once more, I had to lean on the Lord as I bowed my head and asked His divine protection over those two precious children. I was assured that He loved them more than I ever could. Letting go meant more leaning on the Lord for us as parents.

At Heather's time to get her license, we lived in Texas and things were different there. During Heather's preparation time for her license, she had a favorite phrase she used when she wanted to practice driving with a parent. Her phrase was, "Need anything from town?" since we lived out in the country.

As we celebrated with her, I most often "needed" her and Buck to run an errand. When she received her license, I made her a blue T-shirt with "Need anything from town?" in silver lettering on the back. Once again, we were on our knees.

It was always exciting to watch our children grow toward adulthood as they struggled to find their way and make decisions. I realize that Buck's calm, cool manner aided the children to make decisions for the rest of their lives as his patience and acceptance was demonstrated through the learning-to-drive experiences. Celebrating their accomplishments was the easy part for me. At the same time, Buck and I prayed God's protection and safety over God's gifts to our love.

Dance Tip 35

Children are our gifts from the Lord. We hold them for a while and then let them go. Remembering they are on loan helps tremendously, but it is so much easier said than done. These exciting times of celebration are reminders of His love for us and His love for them.

How has parenting increased your lean on the Lord?

Bruce's Graduation Party

I n heading toward Bruce's graduation time, money was a question mark as Buck's company seemed to have trouble deciding whether or not it would pay its work crew. Funds were stretched thin as the added expenses of graduation pictures, invitations, cap and gown rental, college application fees, etc. became a reality.

How could we honor Bruce's accomplishment and let him know how proud we were of him? We discussed what he'd like, and he said he'd just like to invite a few special friends over rather than have a big blowout. We sent out invitations to his special friends, baked a cake, served punch, and waited for his guests.

Lots of people dropped by, from the special adults in his life who had been a great influence as well as many of his high school friends who had not been invited but who wanted to share in Bruce's fun time. Small. Intimate. Just right!

Dance Tip 36

Bruce taught us a lot about life. He taught us to value relationships, to be selective, and to treasure those very special people God presents to you in life. His party was reflective of all of that combined: value, select, treasure. Just right!

Are you valuing those around you? How do you make your selections? What treasures do you celebrate in the friends God has placed in your path as a couple?

Bruce—off to College

After years of hard work and challenging moves back and forth across the United States, Bruce graduated from Vero Beach High School in 1989. Those junior and senior years were interspersed with checking out colleges, looking at possibilities, and his deciding on Brevard College in Brevard, North Carolina.

The summer before college was filled with varied emotions: joy and excitement at Bruce's accomplishment and anticipation as he was about to step into the next stage of independence. As parents, we choked back tears at the thought of our family stepping into a new dimension with incredible adventures ahead.

One day I went into Bruce's room to talk with him, and of course out of my deep love for my firstborn, I was teary. I told him I loved him and it was just hard being a mom right then. He said it was hard for him too, but that he wasn't dying! He was just going to school. (Bruce was always the one to keep things lighthearted and cheerful.)

My mother's heart was filled with so much emotion. I had been teary prior to Bruce's departure. He spent that summer working for our friend's landscaping firm in the daytime and often building model airplanes in his room in the evening. The room was covered with sawdust from shaping and sanding balsa, and it was often filled with fumes from glue and paint. I learned to close the door and treasure his presence more than insisting on orderliness—which would previously been my norm. Why had it taken me so long to learn this concept?

As we packed both cars to begin our venture to Brevard, North Carolina, we would take turns riding with Bruce in his car so each of us could get some special one-on-one time with him. Everything fit just right into those two small Hondas.

We arrived at the school, and Bruce checked in to find out what to do when. We unloaded the two cars at his dorm room and attended a parent meeting with the faculty while the students attended an orientation event.

At that point we made sure that his room was in some sort of order. Then he had another student event to attend.

As we gave our last hugs in his room, God impressed me with this thought: *He's mine now. You've done your part. I'll take it from here.* He knew I needed His reassurance, and He allowed me to leave my son without a tear. Instead I was washed in His peace, knowing our son was in His love and protection.

Dance Tip 37

Emotions can overwhelm us as life presents changes. We all entered this time with confidence in the Lord and what He was doing. However, emotion proves we are still human and needy. How we handle those emotions determines our next steps on life's stage.

What are you two now facing as a couple where you need the Lord's assurance of His profound love and sufficiency?

Honesty Wins!

D uring one of our aerospace layoffs, Buck secured employment in Largo, Florida, but only for three months. Since we had been three months without a paycheck, we had no money to get from Texas to Florida to report for this job. The Lord provided.

We packed what we would need from our Texas house for the three months—things like a coffeepot, an electric skillet, table settings for four (in case the kids came), a card table and chairs, a three-inch foam mattress, bedding, and clothes onto our truck, and off we went. We made it to Largo, registered at a motel and began looking for an apartment, since staying at a motel stay was not financially feasible during this three-month assignment.

As Buck checked into work, I began the apartment search. When I'd call and tell them we were only going to be there for three months, most of them would not lease for less than six months. I continued the search—calling, driving to different complexes, talking to them, and telling of our circumstances. One complex after another turned us down.

We prayed and asked the Lord to just please lead us to the one He had for us. We were not willing to lie by signing a six-month lease and then leaving at the end of only three months. We asked Him to honor our hearts and let us find favor.

On the third night there, after work, we went to dinner and passed by a lovely apartment complex about a mile from his work. We drove up to the office, praying to the Lord that this might be a possibility. When we walked in, the leasing manager who was working late that night met with us and listened to our story. She also asked us to begin filling out our paperwork.

As we completed the paperwork, Buck explained our situation. She said they only offered a six-month and a one-year lease like all the other places. Buck told her we could say we were going to be there six months, and then we would leave in three, but that would not be honest or the right thing to do. After explaining the job shopper opportunity and that his job required him only to be there those three specific months, she told us she would draw up a three-month lease for us since we had told her the truth. She would welcome our stay.

We knew God had honored our truthfulness and we found favor. We would *not* compromise the truth about our circumstances. We found that when we walk in His ways and live our lives in accordance with His ways, He provides what we need. It wasn't us. It was Him and for His glory, perhaps as a witness to the leasing agent.

Dance Tip 38

Many people throughout our ministry years have shared with us how they have "beat the system." They think they have won, but they can never figure out why things just don't seem to work in their favor. Did you ever compromise what you knew was right and then felt that nudge you should not have done it? Buck's motto was always "Do everything as unto the Lord." No compromise. It's all about Him. It's not about us.

How is He getting the glory in all aspects of your lives?

Our Apartment in South Florida—Oh My!

"**O**ut of work" often took on many facets in Buck's aerospace engineering career. One more time, God had allowed that status to be placed before us to teach and grow us in faith and flexibility. Buck found a job in Deerfield Beach, Florida, and we moved to a two-bedroom apartment in Coral Springs.

When we received our last paycheck from Buck's employer, we decided to use it to set up a new bank account and deposited it in a south Florida bank. When we later needed to withdraw some money from our account since we had no cash, we found out they had placed a ten-day hold on our funds since the funds were from a different bank. We had the opportunity to learn some new vibrant dance steps as we tried to exist for days with nothing.

New friends at school for Heather included a friend with no arms or legs. What joy we received as we listened to her eagerness to share in helping her new friend! Bruce's boyhood adventures stretched as he and his friend enjoyed hikes in the woods; the boys had great adventures there.

We found a church family there. We sang in the choir, enjoyed Sunday school, and attended a seminar with several church friends. Once again, we thought we were settled only to find the company needed Buck for only two months. How did we learn this fact? Buck found out by going to work on Thursday, only to find out that Friday would be his final day at work because the contract had ended. As you might imagine, we would have preferred to side step this part of the adventure, but it was not part of the Lord's plan for us.

Care to dance anyone?

We began sending out Buck's résumés and waited on the Lord's provision. We had no money except his last paycheck, but we made it stretch like a rubber band. As we continued to send out the résumés,

Buck received a phone call from a firm in California inviting him out for an interview. Wow—California, here we come! I don't think either of us believed we'd ever get to move to California.

Guess what? The interview went very well. A salary of something was certainly better than nothing, and the Lord guided our every step. While Buck was in California for the interview, he attended our ministry's group leadership meeting there. He was accepted and welcomed with open arms.

However, before we could make the move across country, we calculated to the penny our out-of-pocket expenses needed for the trip. Those expenses came to $989 for motel stays, food, and driving two cars across country. We prayed to the Lord but did not ask anyone for any money. The company would reimburse us once we got to California, but we had to have the money in hand to travel. We waited on the Lord and trusted Him to provide.

One day when I checked the mail, there was an envelope from Buck's mother. The envelope contained a check in the amount of $300, though we had not mentioned anything to her about our finances. (This was out of the ordinary because she never gave us money except small amounts for Christmas or birthdays.) The church gave us a check for $150. Our Sunday school class had also sent along an offering, though I don't remember the amount. Friends of ours from St. Louis sent us a check for $450. Their business was doing very well, and the Lord laid it on their hearts to help us. I don't remember where the rest of the money came from, but I vividly remember that on the morning we left for California, we had $989 to get us across the country to California -- the exact amount we had calculated we would need for our trip.

We packed picnic items for our meals along the way and set out on our cross-country adventure in two cars. I remember some of the highlights of the United States: the palms of Florida, the marshlands and bayous of Louisiana, and rain, *lots* of rain. We saw cotton harvesting in Alabama and Mississippi. I remember eating at a steakhouse in Houston where the waitresses were dressed like cowgirls, and the steak was the best I'd ever eaten! (Maybe our steaks tasted so good because it was our first meal of eating out on the trip!)

Another highlight was that of our time in Fort Stockton, Texas. We crossed what seemed like mostly desolate territory between Houston and

Fort Stockton. We reached Fort Stockton around 10:00 p.m. when we pulled into the Holiday Inn. Their kitchen was closed, so we went exploring to find something to eat. We found a local diner and ordered hamburgers for everyone. We didn't realize Texas hamburgers often came with lots and lots and lots of mustard! Oh well, welcome to Texas!

We traveled from Fort Stockton on toward Los Angeles where we encountered Los Angeles traffic. Driving two cars without cell phones or any type of communication device between us proved to be rather panicky. Bruce and I lost Buck and Heather in his car in downtown Los Angeles, and we had no idea how or if we'd connect up again. I prayed. On Highway 5 north of Los Angeles near Ventura, we connected and drove up Highway 5 in tandem to the San Francisco area, our new home.

We contacted Buck's cousin to stay overnight for our first night, and then we went on to our motel the following day. Four people, two beds, one desk, one small bath for two solid weeks made for coziness. While Buck reported for work orientation, the kids and I had the task of finding a place for us to live.

Dance Tip 39

When we place our lives in the Lord's hands, we must also place our provision there as He fills every need we face. Over and over we saw Him provide when life's circumstances told us things seemed impossible. We serve Jehovah-jireh, Our Provider. He doesn't always provide our wants, but He always provides our exact needs.

As you worship Him, thank Him for His provision no matter how impossible the circumstances seem. In everything, give thanks.

In what ways are you thanking Him for His provision today?

EXCERPT 40

Son Overboard—*Almost*

As we ventured across the United States on the way to our new residence in California, we had driven miles and miles and were ready to do a free day of exploring and seeing some of the sights. We took a drive off the highway through the desert where we saw cactus, jackrabbits, cowboys, and a real Indian on horseback on our way to the Hoover Dam. What a magnificent sight! It's a huge body of water in the middle of the desert, and it was quite an education for Bruce and Heather.

As we were walking along the concrete passageway to get a better view of the dam, Bruce decided he was too short to see. He jumped up onto the waist-high concrete wall and pivoted on the edge. In an instant, Buck reached up and grabbed him by the belt loop of his jeans as he was about to teeter over the forward edge and into the water below. He couldn't see over the edge—he had just wanted to get a better look.

How heart stopping! It was a great response of a dad to save his son— just like our Father reaches out to save us through His Son.

Dance Tip 40

Salvation comes one way: through God the Father through Jesus Christ, His Son. We are reminded how very much He loves us as we are reminded of this father's love for his son.

Are you teetering on the edge, or do you rest in the Father's love as He has rescued you from the wages of sin and death?

EXCERPT 41

The Dance of Submission

A s a wife, I learned a very valuable lesson the hard way. It was the dance of submission.

After about a week and a half looking around for living provisions in California, Buck suggested that the kids and I take the day off and just spend the day at the motel room playing games, relaxing, etc. He said that we should not go out but just stay at the motel. While I appreciated his suggestion, I decided we could just go on a very short trip to see one particular area and return by the time he got home from work. That way, we'd save him some footwork and time that evening. After all, it was only about a twenty-minute drive from the motel, and the kids and I had nothing else to do that day.

We got a map and started to look at all there was to see. As we proceeded closer to our destination, we went down under the overpass and just as we started up the other side, our right rear tire went flat. We were in the middle lane close to the median. Ordinarily this would not be a big deal. However, our station wagon was not only loaded with luggage for the move, the car also contained such valuables as our computer, vacuum cleaner, mops, paper goods, tools, my husband's RC airplanes, cleaning supplies, and toys and games for the kids. There was barely enough room in the car for the kids and myself. We had packed our car full of everything we might need to move into our new apartment.

I prayed and sent Bruce to a neighborhood house to use the phone to call Buck's cousin. No one was at home. He came back and helped me begin to empty out the contents of our car while we were sitting on the inside lane of six lanes of traffic—cars and cars passing us in the pouring rain. A gentleman finally stopped to help this family stranded in the zooming traffic. He not only changed the tire, he helped us unload and load our items to get to the spare. Once that tire was changed, we were on the road back to the motel to wait for Buck, to tell him our story and to go together to find the apartment we were to settle into during our California time.

Buck listened to our tale, gave us all a hug, and went to check the tire to see that it was secure for his family's next adventure. We drove around that night, found the apartment, and were able to sign the lease for our new home.

Dance Tip 41

There is value in submission. It teaches us to place "self" aside and to seek to follow the leadership of the Lord. In learning to dance, there has to be one who leads and one who follows in order for both to enjoy the grace and finesse of the dance. If two people lead, they end up tangled, going in opposite directions. After stepping on each other's toes, feelings, and territories, the dance does not turn out to be as graceful as when there is a leader and a follower.

Submission does not mean dominance. The expression of submission in Ephesians 5 is followed by the words, "as unto the Lord." Submission takes on a whole new meaning contrary to the world's interpretation when we submit to each other as we submit "as unto the Lord."

What does your dance in your marriage look like? Are you dancing with grace and finesse, or are you both pulling and tugging and fighting for the lead? What does the concept of "submission" look like in your marriage? Is it strictly in the world's definition of dominance, or is it in the Lord's example of love and service?

The Sons' Shuffle

Our California move happened between the holiday seasons of Thanksgiving and Christmas. In fact, we found the apartment in Cupertino as we spent two weeks in the area looking for a suitable and reasonable place. After we all looked at it again and signed the lease, we prepared our new apartment for the arrival of our furniture.

The plumbing under the sink was most interesting. Instead of regular plumbing pipes, we found there was a large piece of automobile radiator hose serving as our plumbing connection.

When we began to clean the stove, we found we had to lift the top of the stove in order to clean it. When I lifted the top, I had to scrape spatula after spatula of congealed grease from that area around the burners.

We did get the apartment cleaned and orderly for the movers to arrive with our furniture and boxes on December 22. My mother-in-law was arriving for the holidays on December 24. The four of us worked and worked to unpack boxes. We placed everything in its place and rushed to get settled for the upcoming visit. What cooperation! By the end of those two days, all boxes were unpacked, the walls were decorated, and we had our Christmas tree up with presents wrapped—we were ready for the holidays. How did we do all that in such a short time? Truly, only the Lord knows!

Our guest arrived with her usual flair: winter coat, white leather boots, and white leather gloves (quite the movie star ambience). I never understood it, but I loved her in spite of it. We had a great visit because we were a little more than exhausted. You see, exhaustion forces you to wind down and take some quiet moments to just enjoy the simple things like love and family and the value of being together!

Dance Tip 42

Strength comes in the most unexpected ways. Taking four leaders and using their strengths together for a common goal seemed to be the only way the Lord could have pulled this particular California move together.

Rather than the pull and tug that often happens in families, how might you as parents assess and direct the strengths of each child plus yourselves to work together as a unit rather than separate entities?

How does He perform the impossible by using all of your strengths together for His common goal?

We Danced in Syncopated Rhythm!

Buck and I and the kids had moved to California due to Buck's job offer and for the ministry to couples as well. The move planted us in a small town where we knew only one family—Buck's cousin and her family. After a time, we began making friends through the ministry, the church, and Buck's work.

One night, I decided to invite a family to join us for dinner on the spur of the moment. It was late afternoon and there was no time to check with Buck, but I knew he wouldn't mind. I thought it would be fun to entertain the couple and their two children.

When Buck walked in from work that night, I greeted him at the door with the news of our invited guests. He smiled and stepped aside to introduce me to his friend from work that he'd also invited to dinner on the spur of the moment. He didn't have time to check with me, because he knew I wouldn't mind.

We had plenty of food, fun, and fellowship. Buck and I also secretly celebrated a meeting of the minds as we danced across the room after spending the evening with our guests!

Dance Tip 43

Syncopated rhythm reached out and grabbed us in sweet surprise on this particular evening. In His Word, God often refers to bringing us together "in one mind." I think that means in the practical sense as well as in the supernatural. It's really all the same now, isn't it?

How has the working of God's hand in both your lives surprised you at the least expected turn of events?

EXCERPT 44

The Catering Dance of the Sons Family

A special time for our family happened when we first attended our ministry meeting with our group in California. A couple had offered to drive us to the meeting. On the way, they needed to stop by their church and attend a very short meeting. Their daughter was getting married, and they wanted to ask if the church would host their daughter's reception. The family had been members of the church all their lives and would have been honored to have the church host this special celebration. This would seem most obvious, right?

We entered the room with our friends and just sat and listened at the meeting. As we listened, we couldn't believe our ears! The church had a huge modern kitchen, a lovely room for the reception, and plenty of people to host the occasion. However the objectors outweighed those in favor. The family left the meeting incredibly disappointed, hurt, and with no alternatives for their event.

As we walked to the car, Buck and I looked at each other and instantly knew our wedding gift to the couple. After a few whispers and nods of agreement, we offered our family of four to cater the reception as our wedding gift to our friends' daughter. They were overwhelmed and thought we had lost our minds!

It was great fun! To begin, our friends arranged for a camper in the reception area at a park nearby, and they hired a banjo band for the entertainment.

Our family invited the mothers of the couple and the bride and her bridesmaids to meet at our house for a quiche lunch and celebration time together the day before the wedding. Buck carried in all the groceries in preparation for our time together. He then took the kids to a movie as we girls shared in our time of memory-making together.

To celebrate, we cut up vegetables for veggie trays and made beautiful watermelon fruit baskets for the reception. With those items, plus the cake and drinks, we catered the reception in the park as the banjo band played during the reception. Buck and I manned the camper at the reception, replenishing the veggie trays, drinks, and fruit baskets. Bruce and Heather monitored the items on the tables.

The four of us danced in quickstep as we served the Lord, made a wonderful bonding memory, and pulled off a sweet success!

Dance Tip 44

Uniting as one, though four, certainly paved the way toward bonding us together in the joy of Lord as we *served* others in His love. Watch for special ways you may be granted the privilege. We didn't make this happen. We just watched for the opportunity God placed before us.

Are you watching?

Heather's Slumber Party/Ministry

After our move to California, Heather seemed extremely comfortable, had met several friends her age, and was eager to share her love for life. One of her major adjustments was her fear of the dark. Shadows on the wall at night projected by streetlights onto the bushes and trees outside her windows turned ordinary greenery into unsightly visions of discomfort.

However, she persevered through the ordeal. In a turn of event planning, we decided to invite her friends for a slumber party in the living room of our new apartment. She and I planned the event—the food, the games, and the movies they would watch. We wanted to make certain there were plenty of interesting activities for Heather and her friends.

The friends arrived one Friday night after school, and the party began with lots of giggles, chatting, storytelling, television, and music. Things later settled down into movie time with lots of laughs. The calm allowed for quiet and finally settled into just girl talk.

Early in the morning, the girls packed up, but they wanted to spend more time together, so they left in the middle of the afternoon after another round of talks, giggles, and games. So fun! After the girls left, Heather had an announcement to make to our family. She was no longer afraid of the dark, because God had used her as a witnessing tool to one of her guests. She proceeded to tell us the story.

As these eight-year-old girls were talking after the movie, one of the girls shared her fear of the dark. Heather told her that she could be free of the fear of the dark by trusting Jesus as her Savior and to trust Him with her whole life. She just needed to pray and accept Him as Savior and Lord. They prayed together and Heather's friend received Jesus into her heart. While they were praying together, Heather realized at the time of prayer that Jesus had taken away her own fear of the dark.

Dance Tip 45

How faithful is the Lord to those who trust in Him! We all learned a very valuable lesson as we began a new phase in our walk in faith and trust in Him. Heather had childlike faith, totally trusting as she submitted to the Lord's leading. She witnessed and He listened.

How has the Lord used the fear you had in your life to be a blessing in another's life for His glory and for freedom in yours?

EXCERPT 46

First Florida Landlord Experience

We had put our Florida house on the market three times with no success. The first time, we decided to use a local real estate lady as our property manager since we were living in California at the time. That turned out to give us some peace of mind for a short time knowing someone was looking after the property while we were away. She rented it to a young family. They started out great, but eventually they started sporadically missing payments. Later, missing payments became the norm. This was unacceptable, especially with the high rent of the California housing market that we were in.

We returned home over Christmas to check out our house, and what a surprise! As we drove past the house on the first morning, we saw their little boy swinging on the curtains across our large picture window. They eventually moved out.

Through a job change, we were able to return to Florida from California. Buck's employer would completely redo the inside of our house since we were not using their housing allowance to purchase a home in the area.

I asked friends to measure all the windows and rooms so I could begin the process of ordering carpet, window treatments, etc. When our friends went to measure, the wife told us she was afraid to place her purse on the counter because there were roaches everywhere from the previous tenants. They were in the oven and even in the refrigerator and freezer.

With measurements in hand, I began locating new carpet, new tile, new blinds, etc. When we returned to Florida, we had temporary housing in Cocoa Beach. That meant we had a forty-five-minute drive back and forth from the motel to our home. To begin the renovations, the kids ripped up the carpet in the whole house and helped strip wallpaper off the walls in the kitchen. We painted the whole inside of the house plus had carpet and tile down in two weeks in order for the movers to deliver our belongings from California. Buck had to work most of the days, so he left us in charge of making the house a home. We did it—taking a couple of days break to play at the beach, building sandcastles, collecting seashells, and swimming in the ocean.

One day while painting in our master bedroom, I remember moving the ladder with a bucket of paint on it, which sent the paint can tumbling toward me. Most of the gallon of paint spilled all over the floor as well as saturating my clothing. What a mess! Thankfully that spill happened prior to the carpet delivery!

Buck changed the locks, checked the mechanical things, trimmed the bushes and trees, and we made it our home once more. After so much moving, the four of us had begun working together like a well-oiled machine. Without Christ, that is impossible! With God, all things are possible.

Dance Tip 46

Challenges may not have crept into your relationship through delinquent renters, roaches in every nook and cranny, or in a gallon of paint artistically dumped all over you in the middle of the bedroom floor. However, they have crept in.

The joy of the Lord is our strength. That strength He provides becomes our joy in all things and a sweet remembrance.

How were those minor irritations received in your relationship? Did they mark the beginning of a major battle that later ensued as more and more irritations were added? How were you two able to celebrate, as the impossible became the possible?

EXCERPT 47

One-Third Rent

We had friends who were often in a unique situation. Both the man and his wife worked, but they were at a very, very low point and needed a place to live.

We prayed and asked the Lord how we might help. We had a house in the area they needed, but we also knew they could not pay the rent we needed to make our house payment for that property.

However, the Lord said, *Rent it to them for one-third the needed amount and watch me do the rest.* Oh my! We stepped out in faith, placed our hands in His, and they lived in our house at one-third the rent till they could get on their feet.

He led, we obeyed, and we were all blessed! What seemed impossible, the Lord made possible, just as He promised!

Dance Tip 47

One more time, we got to see the Lord's hand outstretched. He met this couple's need at the moment, gave us the joy of serving, and rewarded us all with an incredible testimony of His sufficiency and His love.

How is the Lord asking you to sacrifice to meet the needs of another?

Blessings in Perfect Timing

We presented a marriage communication weekend to the military at Travis AFB. Friday night's presentation went well, and everything seemed in order. On Saturday morning, all had gone smoothly. After lunch, I went into the restroom before my presentation to the women first thing that afternoon. As I entered the ladies room, there was a woman dissolved in tears, absolutely devastated. In boldness, I asked her if there was anything I could do, and I asked to pray with her. I specifically asked if there was abuse involved. This was a very *bold* statement coming out of my mouth that I knew had not come from me. She said, "No physical abuse."

She shared with me she really liked the seminar because it had so many helps for them as a couple, but her husband was not going to allow them to stay for the remainder of the seminar. He was totally opposed to everything we presenters were teaching. His mind was closed, and he just sat staring and unengaged throughout the seminar.

I prayed with her for the Lord's strength and comfort for her. We also prayed that the Lord would allow them to stay through the next presentation. Buck would be addressing a very important training for the husbands while I would lead the presentation for the wives. She thanked me for praying with her, but she said it would take the Lord to convince her husband to stay.

We continued the afternoon presentation, focusing on the various teachings, breakout sessions, etc. To end the day, we challenged the couples to grow in the Lord together, and we ended with prayer. As we watched the couples leave the meeting room, I looked over and saw the lady I had met earlier. She and her husband walked arm in arm with a big gleaming smile on her face. It made my heart sing! The Lord showed up!

We later received a note from this couple thanking us for the weekend. They asked us to continue to pray as they worked through major issues in the relationship. They expressed the desire to keep in touch.

One year later, we were scheduled for a second seminar at Travis AFB. We contacted this couple to pray as we prepared. We asked them also to pray for all the couples that would attend the upcoming event.

To our surprise, on the first evening as we opened the event, the husband of this couple stood to affirm the choice the couples had made to attend this seminar. He told how much it had helped them, and he asked God's blessing on the event. In addition, they stayed to participate in each presentation during the weekend as a "do over" to glean as much as they could from the teachings. What a blessing!

As the seminar ended, Buck and I were invited to their home and later out to dinner for the evening. The Lord had blessed His Word in the lives of this couple. He also blessed the four of us with a lifelong connection all because of His great love and perfect timing!

Dance Tip 48

In the lives of this couple at the beginning of this seminar, they came with no hope. Then the Lord met them where they were, and He dealt with them to grow them as He led. We did nothing. We were His vessels who had the privilege of watching Him do what He does best. He provides hope and encouragement, restores dreams, and changes the "I" focus to the "we" focus. We stand in awe of His power and His strength and His might!

How is He meeting your need for hope today? In what ways do you two need to surrender to His will to accomplish all He wants for your lives? Are you replacing the "I" thinking with "we" thinking?

Driving Lessons

I t takes a very special personality topped with loads of patience to teach someone to drive under normal teen experience circumstances. We decided to take a different and unique approach to this parental challenge. We decided Bruce and Heather would learn to drive at ten years of age. They would be able, in an absolute emergency, to understand how the car works, how to handle it, and to drive safely if the need arose.

We had an empty area of a subdivision close to our house that had roads but no houses yet. Since Buck was the one blessed with amazing amounts of patience, he suggested the kids do Dad's driver training in a stick shift.

He took the kids back to the subdivision, put them in the driver's seat, and explained the steps of starting the car, braking, clutch work, and shifting gears. Then the driving process began: starting the car, putting it in gear, driving forward, using signals, turning to the left, turning to the right, and stopping. Next came reverse, brakes, shifting, etc.

Driving lessons consisted of hours and hours, done a few minutes at a time. There was lots of jerking, as coordination was developed to increase pressure on the pedal while pressure was released from the clutch. This process was such a treat for both children. I got to hear the excitement in Bruce's calm, cool, collected manner and to see his shoulders straighten. He even seemed to stand a little taller as he worked through the great sense of accomplishment. He was ten years old and could drive a car!

Heather's experience was even more unique. We had moved from subdivision living to apartment living in California by the time she was ten years old. The driving experience for Heather took place in a bank parking lot in the evenings or on Sunday afternoons. Heather was smaller and could barely see over the steering wheel. For hours and hours over several months, our little green Honda Civic jerked forward to a smooth progress, stopping quite abruptly as her short legs worked to develop the finesse of her coordinating movements from the gas pedal to the brakes.

There was always lots of laughter together as Dad and daughter returned to the apartment from their "drive." I was very impressed at Heather's eagerness to follow instructions.

Buck never once criticized the kids' skill as they were learning. He never made fun of them or demeaned them in their times of learning a new skill. He showed them value and respect as unique individuals. He always found something positive at the end of their sessions to share as a compliment with them. I got to cheer them on and provide the celebration during the process.

Dance Tip 49

Life presents a number of challenges as we move forward in the process of marriage. It often requires patience through jerky awkwardness to eventual finesse and polish as we grow and learn the steps toward oneness in Jesus' love. No condemnation; no criticism. Love is patient and kind (1 Corinthians 13). Rejoice in the process toward finesse only the Lord can provide.

In what ways are you learning a new process that takes "baby" steps?

When Bruce Became a Man!

It was hard for Bruce during our move to California. We moved in the middle of the year. Class friendships had been formed at the junior high, connections had been made in clubs, etc. Bruce was sad and down in the dumps—he had no friends and was lonely.

We prayed with him and waited for God's provision in friends. He came home from school a couple of weeks later so excited! He had a paper from his teacher inviting the science class parents to a meeting for a week trip to Yosemite. We attended the meeting eagerly.

God, on that evening, provided a friendship for Bruce with a young man who was his roommate for the trip. The guys had a tremendous, fun adventure: biking in the snow and rain, dealing with snow that came up to the windowsill of the cabin, crawling on their hands and knees through the spider caves, and moving residences from the lower valley to a cabin farther up the mountains through the snow in the middle of the week.

When Bruce arrived home from the trip, he very politely asked us about our activities of the week. As we shared with him our events, he sat patiently and listened out of thoughtful consideration.

When we finished, Bruce eagerly shared with us how boring our week had been compared to his. He announced he'd become a *man*! He was now responsible. He could pack. He could move residences on his own. And most of all, he shared that he could have a great time doing it. He was a man now at twelve, and it was important for us to realize his new status.

This was a new dance in the steps of parenthood!

Dance Tip 50

Growth is not always pleasant. There is pain involved (like biking in the snow and rain). Oftentimes, when things look the worst, God shows up to encourage us with a magnificent surprise that is much better than we could ask or think.

What growth has been presented in your relationship, and how has He shown up to surprise you in the midst of your pain?

EXCERPT 51

Travis AFB—Group Fears Discussion

Buck and I learned a dancing lesson at a Travis AFB time with the military. During one of our events there, we divided the couples into small groups for discussions. As we walked from group to group, we overheard a topic that stirred our attention because it certainly applied to the dance steps of a marriage.

The topic of discussion came about as one man talked about his approaching retirement date from the military. He shared that he had sent out résumés and set up interviews. The discussion eventually headed toward fear of the unknown. He shared with the group that he had served in the military since he left high school. All his adult life, he'd known the military life. He shared that in the military, you're teamed together, and you *know* that the man or woman next to you is going to cover your back no matter what, whether at war, at peace, in a foxhole, on the battlefield, or in your office. The person next to you will lay down his life for you.

As he now approached life in the world outside the military, the tendency of many people to climb over anything and everything and everyone to achieve any measurable success seemed like a totally foreign concept to him. In fact, it struck a tremendous sense of fear in him that left him visibly "shaking in his bootstraps."

What Buck and I learned was that the Lord had given us a gift of His love! We shared God's Word regarding His faithfulness to us, His children. Buck and I had not served in the military. The Lord had strengthened us by leading us to wonderful friends and co-workers with our nine moves in seventeen years back and forth across the United States. He had provided many wonderful friends in the fellowship of the family of Christ. Just as He promised, He had never left us nor forsaken us. In fact, those moves were often used to draw us to Him, then to each other for His strength and provision when we had none.

We encouraged this man to read God's Word, to cling to God's Word and His promises, and to cling to his wife. We challenged him to place his hand in the Lord's to begin his new adventure in faith, believing and walking in Him. In Him, he would find His strength, teamed with his wife.

Dance Tip 51

Trust is a huge word and has an incredible impact in a husband/wife relationship. Are you sensitively or selectively hearing your mate's needs and wants? Are you both clinging to God's Word and listening as the Holy Spirit nudges as you dance through life?

Do you walk in lockstep through all situations, drawing close to the Lord and to each other, or are the circumstances of life used as "trips and stumbles" to throw you both off balance?

As you dance in this relationship called marriage, have you practiced the steps that will lead to confidence in the midst of the fear? Do you rest assured your partner has your back, no matter what?

EXCERPT 52

God Sent an Angel named Bob!

After a year or so in California, my breathing just didn't seem to cooperate. As an asthmatic, I was struggling, but I just thought the change in weather and surroundings would be something my body would eventually tolerate.

One night at a ministry meeting, one of the girls, who had been a nurse, noticed I was having difficulty breathing. She looked at my fingernails (which were turning blue at the base) and told me my system was not getting enough oxygen. She said if it did not rain in the next couple of days, I needed to get some oxygen. We were in the drought period of the year in that particular area, but I heeded her warning and prayed. Two nights later, we had a huge thunder and lightning storm that never happened at that time of year in California! I said a "thank You" and went about my routine.

Within that week, Buck "happened" to see a friend at his work he had not seen since the day he arrived in California. The friend asked him how our family was settling into our new life in the west. Buck told him the kids were doing well in school, but I was having breathing problems and probably would not be able to stay in the area for a lengthy time. The friend, named Bob, suggested my husband come to his office at the end of the day.

At that late-day meeting, Bob mentioned to Buck there was a position opening back in Florida. That position needed a person who had developed the program in California and who could follow it through and implement the complete program at the Cape. Buck was that person. He said he would make the arrangements for our transfer within the month.

God is amazing to meet our every need when we call on Him. It's not that He sent us back to Florida, which did most certainly happen. But if He had needed Buck to stay in California, He would have met our needs there too. He cares. We were eager to give God the glory! Once more, we were on our way.

Dance Tip 52

Your circumstances are not identical to ours, but the Lord is at work within your scenario to bring about His plans. Ask Him, thank Him, and count on Him!

How is the Lord working behind the scenes to meet your every need as a couple and as a family?

Do You Remember?

O ur adventure began shortly before Thanksgiving when the man who was renting to own our Florida house called to say he was unable to make the payments and that we could have the house back. As soon as Buck hung up the phone, he turned to me and said, "Do you remember?" My reply was, "I remember. What do you think this means?"

We were referring to a late-night walk we had taken as a family while we were visiting Florida on vacation from California. We had flown in over the Christmas holidays to take care of a plumbing problem there at the house. I was studying Genesis in Bible Study Fellowship. I had learned that part of preparing Abram to receive God's covenant was the walk in the land, and everywhere his feet touched, God would give that land to him and his seed (Genesis 13:14–18).

Taking the Lord literally, Buck and I and the kids walked that land near our home and claimed it for Christ, saying that everywhere we stepped our foot, to the north, to the south, to the east, and to the west, we claimed that land. There is power in God's Word.

After our stint in aerospace in California, we returned to that house and area once again and lived for five years. After that, due to a forced job reduction, we moved to Texas and rented the house to friends for four years. Later when those friends no longer needed the house, we sold it (rent to own) on contract to the current renter. Then after renting the house for three years, we got it back.

Immediately our thoughts began to ask if the Lord needed us back in that house and area in ministry for Him. We watched as He unfolded every detail. First, our friends in Colorado were praying for us as they did each morning, and they were impressed to send us a page from their devotional. They said they didn't know how or why it related to our lives, but they knew the Lord needed that page sent to us. This devotional page was entitled, "Going—Not Knowing." The writing talked about Paul standing up and pointing south (Florida is certainly south!) and recalling the covenant God gave to Abraham.

Buck submitted his résumé to the three Florida companies where he'd previously worked. We prayed that if the Lord wanted us there, it was in His hands. We'd done all we could do. Now we had to wait.

Buck, Bruce, and I made a trip to that area over the Christmas holidays to assess and do whatever work was necessary. We painted and did some major repairs. Through a lady in our church, we were given Haggai 2:9: "The glory of this latter house shall be greater than of the former, said the Lord of hosts; and in this place will I give peace, saith the Lord of hosts" (KJV).

The following week, we were given the following Scriptures:

I will instruct thee and teach thee in the way which thou shalt go: I will guide thee with mine eye. (Psalm 32:8 KJV)

And David said to Solomon his son, Be strong and of good courage, and do it: fear not, nor be dismayed: for the Lord God, even my God will be with thee; he will not fail thee, nor forsake thee, until thou has finished all the work for the service of the house of the Lord. (1 Chronicles 28:20 KJV)

But the anointing which ye have received of him abideth in you, and ye need not that any man teach you: but as the same anointing teacheth you of all things, and is truth, and is no lie, and even as it hath taught you, ye shall abide in him. (1 John 2:27 KJV)

And a vision appeared to Paul in the night; There stood a man of Macedonia, and prayed him, saying, Come over into Macedonia, and help us. And after he had seen the vision, immediately we endeavoured to go into Macedonia, assuredly gathering that the Lord had called us for to preach the gospel unto them. ... And on the Sabbath we went out of the city by a river side, where prayer was want to be made: and we sat down, and spake unto the women which resorted thither. (Acts 16:9–10, 13 KJV) (Sebastian is a city on the river, and Disney had just built a big new resort there.)

While we were painting and repairing, we prayed and kept asking the Lord to show us His path. We had released this property and the idea of living in Florida when we sold the house. However, we only wanted what the Lord wanted, not our wants. Shortly before we left the state, a young couple came to us and asked if we'd rent the property on a month-to-month basis. He had just graduated from Bible school and was waiting for His next step like we were. (Sounded so familiar.) So, we looked at that as the Lord's provision for them and for us, and we returned to work. However, we *knew* the Lord's "pull" on our lives was returning to Florida soon. How would it all come together?

A week later, that young couple called to say they would not be renting. Another door had opened for them, but they thanked us for our consideration.

We continued to seek the Lord and decided not to call the three companies where Buck had submitted his résumé. Buck's prayer request and heart's desire was that he would finish his career with one particular company at the Cape, but more than that, he wanted God's desire for us. We had talked about this just the night before and made the decision not to call but to wait on the Lord. We waited.

The very next day, we had a message on our answering machine that the Cape had called and wanted to talk to Buck about his résumé. When he called, they set up an interview for January 24, our twenty-eighth wedding anniversary. What a gift!

We flew to Orlando on January 23, rented a car, and drove to our hotel on Cocoa Beach. There we met friends for dinner and checked on our house in Sebastian. The Lord provided perfect weather, upgraded accommodations to a villa with a beach view, and even included a full moon on the ocean. It was the perfect setting to rejoice in our love and years together and to praise our heavenly Father for His provision!

We could see God's hand stamped over every detail of our trip. (For instance, we had reserved a Holiday Inn room on the beach, per the company's instruction, but none were available when we arrived. We were upgraded to a villa for one-half the price of the beach room. With Buck's "buy one night, get one night free" coupon, we had a $249/night room for the two nights for a total of $52.)

During the interview, all his friends welcomed him back so joyously. They threatened to cut off the interviewer's supply of donuts if they didn't hire Buck back. They said the grapevine had been buzzing with "Buck's coming" for days. The interview went very well, but they could only make a recommendation to the California facility. California was in charge of all hiring. We waited—trusting, confident, and eager!

Dance Tip 53

Things don't always go as we plan. However, when we, as couples, seek the lordship of Jesus Christ and surrender to Him and Him only, things tend to go His way, which is always much better than we could ever imagine. The key here is the surrender not only to Jesus as Savior, but even more, to the lordship of Jesus Christ in every area of our lives.

When we marry, we are not concerned only about ourselves. We are to work together as a team. As the Lord's handiwork, we seek a new and different path than when we were in the world. Explore the difference of Jesus as Savior and Jesus as Lord.

Have you two made the switch from Jesus as Savior to Jesus as Lord in your individual lives and in the couple relationship you call "marriage"?

Texas Move—$1,000 Gift

I n a previous chapter, I shared how the Lord moved us to Florida to start the marriage ministry there. While my husband was working at that job location, he met up with a colleague he had worked with at a previous location. They were both amazed to be working together in Florida, and now in Texas years later.

This friend and his family had moved to Texas a couple of years prior to our locating there. They had settled in, liked the schools, and were a great help in answering all our many questions about the area. The guys worked, met occasionally for lunch, and often found laughter a big relief for the stresses of the aerospace memories as well as the current workload.

When they both received their layoff notice along with 898 other people from their firm, they often met to discuss new job-hunting strategies. They carpooled fifty miles into Dallas to use the Dallas library in their job searches, and they helped each other on house repairs, etc.

One day we had a surprise visit from this friend. He came out to our house for a glass of tea and to "shoot the breeze." With no discussion of finances, though it had been over two months since the guys had been out of work, this friend pulled out his checkbook and wrote my husband a check for $1,000. There was no explanation. We tried to turn it back to him, but he would not hear of it. He knew we needed it with our two children in college.

God provided through a very dear friend, as a surprise of His faithfulness!

Dance Tip 54

We truly had no idea how we would meet our house payment that third month plus pay the other bills. The Lord knew, and He provided before we even asked. Once again, we stood amazed and humbled at how much He cares about every detail.

We were blessed by a "divine surprise" in the form of a gift of $1,000 on that hot, summer Texas day. He met our need truly as we walked on His path—even from the most unlikely provision. His ways are truly not our ways. For that, we rejoice!

How is He meeting your needs through gifts from the most unlikely place?

EXCERPT 55

"Hot Tub Trauma"

I decided to provide Heather with a gift before she left for college. I surprised her by vacuuming out her car and detailing it for her new adventure. In that process, I turned "just right to be wrong." I ended up in severe back pain over the next couple of months and was under chiropractic treatment.

During my Texas back pain, I realized that getting into the hot tub (though we used it with cool water in the summer) felt so great for my back. Of course it wasn't hard to convince Buck to enjoy a time of relaxing in his favorite spot on our Texas property after a long hard day at work.

One morning, as my back had improved considerably, I decided to go out and enjoy some water time. I got out of the house, climbed the steps to get into the tub, and was enjoying my time in the sun. The day was sunny, traffic past our house was light, and the big Texas sky was true to form—*big*! The sky was the bluest blue ever!

As I decided it was time to get back to work in the house, I realized there was one major problem. I tried to get up out of the tub and found that my muscles were not strong enough for me to stand up. I tried multiple times but could not stand up or climb the steps up and out of the tub. What was I going to do? I had no cell phone at that time, and there were no neighbors close enough to recognize my predicament.

I began to pray and ask the Lord for His help. I tried again and just could not get enough muscle strength to make it out of the tub. My back muscles were too weakened by the recent injury. I had been praying quietly, not out loud. However, as my dilemma lengthened, I began praying out loud that the Lord would handle this situation.

As I was praying out loud with my back to our house, Buck came in the side gate and over to the tub. He asked what was going on. While I no idea there was anyone near me, I was *so* relieved to see him. He had not planned to come home for lunch that day (we were one mile away from his work), but he just needed a break and decided to spend some time with me. I cried and cried because I was so thankful for his coming as God's answer to my prayer. When I explained my situation to him, he agreed God had used him to help.

While my back muscles wouldn't allow me to dance for several more weeks physically, in my heart I danced before the Lord as He had sent my partner-in-life to rescue me and to be my real "down-to-earth" hero!

Dance Tip 55

God's surprises have been incredible over the years. This one was a true lifesaver. He knew my need and answered it by laying it on Buck's heart to take a break and drive home for lunch with his wife. In the ordinary, that is such a little thing! That day, God's heart matched Buck's heart to meet mine.

How does He meet your needs through your mate through the little things that make you want to dance?

EXCERPT 56

Heather to College

Heather's leaving for college was just as hard, but totally different than our experience with Bruce had been. Her senior year was filled with several activities in our Texas town with lots of new friends and planning her graduation events.

Since many of our friends and family lived out of state and we had only lived in Greenville a short time, Buck and I wondered what we might do to make Heather's graduation celebration really special.

We came up with an idea to send a request to all family and friends across the United States. We requested each family send a picture and a letter sharing with Heather a special memory of her in their lives or something they appreciated about Heather. We mailed the requests in February and received so many replies that we incorporated them into an album. We presented it to her along with her additional gifts.

What a fun, surprised look she had on her face as she opened the gift and began to read the encouragement and love across the miles. She read and read, but she let us know she'd read the last letters written by Bruce, Dad, and me located at the end of the book in the privacy of her room because she knew she would cry.

In the process of working toward Heather's move to her college, I decided to clean out her car as a special surprise. With that activity, I was left in excruciating pain in the chiropractic office, and later unable to sit in a chair or on the couch. The floor became my resting place for months as I ate my meals, talked with friends, helped with college entrance exams for Heather and her friends, played games with the family, and watched a little TV. I could not stand on my feet to cook, could not clean, and did little to contribute to the household. Buck took the lead as chief cook (carry in) and the one who cleaned, and in his great love, he tolerated this major inconvenience in our lives. He took Heather shopping for college supplies. That was something I had so looked forward to doing, but it was not possible. They packed the cars as I watched in pain and frustration that I couldn't participate.

It was so hard as a mother to see her baby step out in independence and freedom that was so absolutely necessary as a young adult. I cried at the front door as they pulled out of our driveway, and I worked my way to the back door to get in one last wave and to pray for God's protection and promises fulfilled in our daughter, Heather.

A mother's love runs so deep, but Buck was also touched as he shared with me about unpacking her car at school, getting her room in order, and the *long* two-hour drive home. The empty nest had begun.

Dance Tip 56

As parents, we wait for our baby's arrival. We love and teach and teach and love them through bicycles, bumps and bruises, first teeth, lost teeth, lost keys, best friends, cruelty in the classroom, driver's licenses, tickets or warnings, prom, and graduation. We trust that someday parenthood will hopefully turn to friendship over the years, with no guarantees.

However, when that last baby leaves the nest, while a new adventure opens for parent and child, parent heart tugs become increased as we realize this is for real now. We train our children because we want them to be strong enough to stand on their own. As parents, we question whether we've forgotten any part of that preparation. And then we pray!

EXCERPT 57

A Car Prayer

Buck volunteered to assist a young man and his family with some much-needed car repair. With two small children and one on the way, combined with the man's minimal salary, needs exceeded funds for this young family. Buck often reminded us that God teaches us that if you have something someone needs, you need to give it away. For Buck, that often meant using his engineering ability combined with mechanical skills to help our friends with various vehicle repairs.

The young gentleman came over one weekend, and Buck prayed silently before he began the work. As Buck proceeded, things were not going well. Once he'd get one thing repaired, that would lead to something else that needed attention. Finally as he got to the final repair, nothing he and his young friend tried worked—absolutely *nothing*!

After trying a number of times, the engine just would not start. Finally Buck looked over at his young friend and asked him if he'd prayed before they started working on the car. His friend gave him a puzzled look. He said, "You mean you pray over a *car*?" Buck answered he prayed over everything. He explained that God is our source of blessing and triumph. Therefore, He wants to be included in all that we do.

The men stopped and prayed together. Guess what? God blessed their time in prayer. As they began work on that car again, everything came together and the car was up and running in no time. Hands covered with black grease were raised in thanksgiving!

Dance Tip 57

Prayer is an invaluable tool in our toolbox of faith … when two or more or gathered in my name … to God be the glory! When we see a resurrected car before our very eyes, we give Him thanks because we placed it in His hands before we started.

Lordship means Jesus is Lord of all, even car repairs, grocery shopping lists, event scheduling, etc.—everything!

Do you pray over everything, because the Lord tells us we are to give thanks in everything?

EXCERPT 58

One Unique Recliner

Our friends—a retired couple living in Colorado—were in need of a recliner. We met in California while we were all living there, and they "adopted" the four of us as their extended family. They were a beautiful, fun-loving couple because they so loved life. We shared so many fun memories like pinochle games, San Francisco v. Dallas football games, and lots of jokes and laughter over the years.

This lady had phoned three weeks earlier to let us know that her husband had been taken to the hospital with double pneumonia and emphysema and was extremely weak. She was having a bout with bronchitis and pink eye and could not visit him because she was so sick. We prayed together, asking for the Lord to intervene and heal. Buck and I really hurt for them since they were sick and alone in their separate places.

A week later, she phoned to say her husband was at home, but he still had the double pneumonia. He had to be rechecked by the doctor in a couple of days, but he had not slept the night before. To get his breath, he had to sit up in a straight chair since they didn't have a recliner. He would need twenty-four-hour oxygen for the rest of his life due to his emphysema and would not be able to return to work again. (He had been working as a custodian at an elementary school when he became ill.)

After we prayed and I hung up the phone, the Lord impressed me to phone the local division offices of a major department store and ask for a recliner for our Colorado friends. I phoned the catalog department and was directed to customer service relationship. I explained this man's health condition and that he was losing sleep because he could not lie in a bed and needed a recliner. I explained the Lord had impressed me to call and ask them for a recliner. I was obeying His instructions.

I also explained that we could not pay for the recliner nor could our friends. I explained I just knew their company had a recliner in a warehouse *somewhere* that hadn't sold, and this man needed it. (Ask and ye shall receive—right?) They said they would check with their Colorado warehouse and get back to me.

Two days later, the company phoned to say they had located a recliner in a Colorado warehouse. They would deliver it to my friends on the following Thursday. I thanked them and explained the necessity of getting to our friend as soon as possible, but whatever they could do would be appreciated.

I phoned the wife to tell her how the Lord had impressed me. When I told her about the phone call I had made, she was overwhelmed. She said she'd never met anyone like me before with that kind of boldness, and she just cried and cried. To quiet the mushiness, which I knew was heartfelt gratitude, I laughed and said, "It may be green plaid, or better yet, purple with orange dots." I mentioned that the color wouldn't really matter if her husband would be more comfortable, right?

She shared with me they were living with their daughter, who was extremely particular about her home décor and that everything *had* to match. We laughed and agreed the Lord was a Master decorator.

Then my friend said that when she had told me about her husband having to sit up at night, she had left out that she had gone in to check on him during the night, and he was sitting up in a straight chair with his head bobbing as he tried to sleep. It broke her heart. Scurrying back to her room, she had dissolved into tears and wondered why he had to suffer. I reminded her that the Lord loved them, and this was all possible just because He knew they needed that chair to make her husband more comfortable.

On Tuesday morning (not Thursday as I was originally told), I got a phone call from our Colorado friends. The Colorado warehouse had delivered to them a brand-new recliner that "just happened" to match *the exact shade of blue* as their daughter's couch, and they wanted to celebrate with me that it had arrived.

She told me the deliveryman kept flipping through the papers on his clipboard, looking for a sales receipt, but he couldn't find one. Her husband told him, "There isn't one. This chair has been sent by the Lord through our friend in Texas, and there was no sale." His reply, "Well, I've never heard of anything like that before in my whole life!"

What a testimony to God's goodness and all sufficiency!

Dance Tip 58

As we danced at God's greatness in such a thing as a much-needed recliner for our friends, His joy has been shared over the years as a testimony to His greatness. We will ever praise Him for the love we saw poured out in the grace of His goodness that in this case, took the form of one unique recliner.

Amazing? *Yes!* Unbelievable? *Yes!* Absolute awe? *Yes!* That *is* the God we serve!

How are you two looking at the impossible instead of believing a God of the possible?

The Birthday Book

Birthdays are often tough to keep as unique and special celebrations of the ones we love. Buck was turning fifty—a milestone in life—and I wanted to make it super special for him. Our moves and missionary travels had taken us to both coasts of the United States, and we'd made many precious friendships. What could I do to include them to celebrate Buck's fiftieth birthday to honor him on this day?

When Heather graduated from high school, I'd sent out letters asking our friends and family to write Heather a note. I had asked them to share a special memory they had shared with her, or pictures, or a Scripture—anything that was special between them and our daughter. As the letters came in, I had collected them into a binder for her very special graduation gift. She had been very touched by their sharing, and that book became a treasured gift in her life.

I decided to do the same thing for Buck's *big fifty*. I wrote the letter, copied it, stuffed the envelopes, and mailed them. I tried to include many friends, coworkers, ministry partners, and family members. About three weeks later, the letters and pictures and cards came pouring in. I assembled them in a leather-bound book.

On September 7, 1995, Buck opened a huge box that included the book. At first, he was amazed that so many people would take the time to write and share with him. He skimmed through it, completely overwhelmed. He truly could not speak.

Later after cake and ice cream, he began to read each contribution. Every night for a week, he'd read more letters after supper, sharing the honor, love, and respect our friends had shown to him through this special gift. That gift was such a treasure!

Buck and I danced through life, sharing and caring for others. Now it was his turn to take a bow with a thankful heart to the One who made it possible.

Dance Tip 59

A time for reflection over the last decade or two or five might be appropriate as you rejoice in His hand reaching out and providing His love just as He promised. Take a moment to give Him thanks and praise and adoration. He stands waiting!

Are you two dancing through life, celebrating with each year of God's love and care?

Parenting Means Trust in the Lord

A t 4:00 p.m. the skies were blue and beautiful over northeast Texas as my daughter's date arrived to take her flying for the first time. This young man seemed very nice and mature, and his instrument rating as well as his private pilot's license assured us of his responsibility and qualifications as a pilot. With confidence, I entered my little motherly reminder—"And you realize, of course, I *am* trusting you with my daughter's *life*"—as they departed. A new and wonderful experience for our Heather was about to happen while I stood wondering if we had made the right decision in giving permission to go.

One of her friends stopped by a little later. She had forgotten about Heather's flying date, and stated, "I can't imagine you letting her go. My parents would never let me do anything like that." This comment only led me to further question the wisdom of our decision.

By 5:00 p.m., the dark clouds had rolled in over that big Texas sky, and the huge raindrops were pelting our patio roof. We prayed for Heather's safety. I knew she was taken care of—because my husband and I had prayed for her safety with her that morning, and the Lord would honor our prayers as always.

As the storm became more violent, my faith seemed to weaken. I stood at our front door with tears streaming down my face, and I realized that there are just times when you have to totally let go. There is *nothing* but trust in the Lord. At other times in my life, trusting the Lord seemed so easy. Today I realized that this was roughest part of parenting Heather, walking in faith and again trusting her care to the Lord, in the sky with a pilot friend I had just met a few times. You see, I was not in control, as parents like to think they are.

Then I reflected back to another time when this loss of control had surfaced in my life ... when my dad lay in the hospital after he was run over by a piece of road construction equipment, and all I could do was pray. I prayed and prayed and prayed that day, only to hear the nurse come to tell us, "He's gone." I had trusted the Lord at that time with his care, but the Lord's answer to my prayer did not match the answer I wanted. I believed in miracles, but that didn't happen in restoring my dad back to a healthy, vibrant life. Instead I had to accept the Lord's answer in death.

I continued to watch the sheets of Texas rain blow across our property. Inwardly, I trembled at every crash of thunder that invaded the privacy of my prayers.

My husband and I had made plans with our son and his girlfriend to go shopping in a town fifty miles away, and I left very reservedly, concerned that if we were needed, we would not be nearby. Where was my faith? One of the blessings the Lord has given to me is the spiritual gift of faith, and yet I seemed so weak in that moment. Within the hour and a half of the horrific rainstorm and dark sky, the rain had dwindled, yet calm was hard to find within myself as I gazed in the direction of the airport and the skies became blackened once more. *"Oh Lord, You are so powerful—I do trust you,"* were my thoughts as we left our driveway. In our weakness, we are made strong in the Lord, not by our own strength, but in His.

The Lord made me reach all the way down inside to pull up all my faith at that time, and yet it wasn't enough. Through this experience, He showed me I do not have what it takes to maintain and that I must be totally surrendered and submitted to His will and His care. I was all of that, I thought—but I felt as if I were just hanging on by a thread.

Heather was my baby, my child, and I found that even though she was almost seventeen, the task of parenting took more faith then than it ever had when she'd cry from an earache or itch with the chickenpox or "strawberry" hives. But just as the Lord pulled me through the anxiety of the little girl limp in my arms from fever and pain then, He was able to comfort my fears and calm the storm inside me now seventeen years later.

I praise Him for being my Father, the one with all the right answers, not just the ones we want. I praise my heavenly Father for a set of circumstances that once again whittled away at "self" within me. "Self" must die, and Christ must be on the throne of our lives. I learned that my faith grows deeper with each circumstance presented in my path. I praise Him for calming the storm outside to assure my daughter's safety as well as calming the storm that raged inside of me. For this, I give Him glory and praise, and I honor Him as my Lord!

Dance Tip 60

Take time to reflect on the words *surrender, lordship, faith,* and *strength* as they are revealed in your life.

When has the Lord demanded more of you than you had to give?

Has He shown you absolute and total dependence on Him as the only way to handle all life has in store? How have you two been able to dance through these storms?

Our Side Steps in Columbus, Georgia

What happens if you throw a party, send out all the invitations, set aside the time, schedule the hall, drive eight hours to the location, and no one shows up? If you recall from earlier experiences shared, this would now be the second time in our ministry this had happened. The first time was at a church. This was at an army facility.

Sure enough, that is what happened as our first ministry weekend assignment with a group we served to minister to military marriages. The base chaplain contacted Buck and me to present the weekend at Fort Benning, Georgia. Food was ordered, arrangements for the room were made, projection equipment was brought in, our travel arrangements were confirmed, reservations by the couples were settled through the chaplain's office, and we were on our way.

We arrived eager to see what the Lord was going to do in the lives of these military couples. We met the base chaplain at the office. He greeted us with an immense apology. He expressed his appreciation in our coming, etc. However, his two units had been called out on an emergency training exercise the afternoon we had arrived. Therefore, there would be no weekend ministry event.

The Lord ordered our steps. We didn't have to understand where or why the circumstances might lead us. We were just willing to go and obey.

Surprise!

Dance Tip 61

We are called to walk in obedience. We do not need to understand nor do plans have to take place as we think they should. It's all about Him. It's not about us.

How is God relating this principle to you two in life or in ministry?

Excerpt 62

Piercing Eyes

As a weekend ministry leadership for the military, we had quite an adventure. Fort Hood was offering a marriage weekend, and Buck and I had been invited to speak. The anticipation began when Buck and I received our assignment months prior to the weekend. We went out to Ft. Hood, Texas, three months prior to the weekend ministry event to make all the necessary arrangements. We were scheduled to meet with the chaplain and with the lieutenant general to plan the details of the upcoming event.

Prior to arriving at Ft. Hood, we'd been assured we would be met and shown to our quarters. We arrived at Ft. Hood at midnight, and no one was at the airport. No one was available to pick us up or to show us to our quarters. We phoned our leadership to see what was up. Our ministry office leadership had planned to contact Ft. Hood but had neglected to do so. Buck and I were civilians and could not make these arrangements ourselves. With a few phone calls, and a couple of hours, etc., arrangements were finally made and we were settled.

The next morning, we met with the chaplain at his office. He was preparing to retire. He was also coming to the reality that his daughter had informed him she could adopt a baby without getting married. He shared with us how disturbed he was over the act of adoption by a single mother would make a man's role considerably insignificant in society. This situation unnerved him prior to our arrival to do our part to preserve marriages within the military. God always knows what is needed in a very perfect time frame.

Later in that planning weekend, we were taken to meet with the lieutenant general of the facility. After a brief introduction, we were left alone with him. His eyes were piercing to the very heart of who we were. His sole focus was on the care of his command.

We answered specific questions such as "What do you teach? What will you tell them re: _____?" He agreed with the answers Buck gave. His concern was that once his guys made captain, the wives were demanding the men leave the army. He needed us to specifically address that issue during the weekend. If God was telling the men to get out, then that was something totally different. But if they were being disobedient to the warrior status God had called them to, how would we address that? When Buck answered and I was asked for my input, the general said he wished us well and would welcome our ministry to his command. Nothing could stand in God's way of His truth getting to His people.

As the couples attended the weekend, one couple came to us at the end of the last presentation. Their comment went something like this: "You two would not have had to say anything this weekend. We have been married nine years and came into this weekend knowing if we continued going the way we were going, we would not make it to number ten. However, by the respect, love, and honor you two showed us this weekend as you maneuvered through these sessions, you proved to us that God's love does sustain us in a marriage. It wasn't what you said. It was how you treated each other."

Dance Tip 62

We never know who's watching and what they are observing in our lives. One thing we know for certain: the Lord had His way at Ft. Hood!

Are you two willing to get out of the way to allow the Lord to reflect His love through you? Who is observing the two of you? How are you two reflecting the Lord in all you say and do to His glory? Are you dancing before the Lord to His glory?

EXCERPT 63

"Paid in Full"

When we paid off a house we owned in 1995, we sent the following letter to the mortgage company:

To you:

Today is a very important day in our lives. We fulfill our commitment to pay off our debt that we owe. For you, it may be just another check in the bank or another collection call you will not have to make or another letter you won't have to write. However, let us assure you, it is the fulfillment of our Lord's promise to us that He would provide for our every need and would give us the desires of our hearts as we followed Him.

In 1980, our Lord Jesus Christ called Buck and me to minister to married couples and families. Since that time, we have had fifteen years of steady preparation, a testing of our faith and commitment to Him, times of no work, health issues, and yet the Lord always promised His provision and blessing if we'd just hang in there.

During these past few months, the Lord has taken us one step further in our walk with Him. He has called us to ministry in Little Rock, Arkansas. One of the requirements to be a missionary with their organization is that we must be debt free. Through a chain of events including losing a job, to our very last twenty-dollar bill, through a temporary job in Florida for two months, and the Lord leading us here to Little Rock, He has provided a way for us to mark this debt, "Paid in Full." With those words and the enclosed check, we rejoice!

However, as we send along this final bill marked, "Paid in Full," we also think of our lives and the debt Jesus paid when He died for our sins and hung on that cross at Calvary for the sin of the world. No greater payment has been offered for the sinful condition of mankind. He gave up His life because He loved us so much. Now He is alive after His resurrection from the grave that could not hold Him, and He will come again to take all who love Him to be with Him someday!

Just as He has loved us, He loves you, too, and He wants you to come to know Him and to trust Him as your Lord and Savior. If you have not asked Jesus to be the Lord of your life, listen to what He might be saying to you today. He never pushes His way in. He only stands at the door and knocks. You must invite Him into your heart. We don't all commit great sins like murder, armed robbery, or that kind of thing. But the Lord says in His Word, the Bible, "All have sinned and come short of the glory of God (Romans 3:20). And He says of Jesus, "I am *the* way, *the* truth and *the* life. No man comes to the Father but by me" (John 14:6).

It's your decision. What will it be? Where do you want to spend eternity, with Jesus who loves you just the way you are, or in hell where there is no love, no hope, and only devastation forever?

Our debt for our sin has been "Paid in Full." How about yours?

In His love and service for the family,
Buck and Lin Sons

Dance Tip 63

We have many opportunities to be a witness for the Lord. We can use a celebration like paying off a mortgage or a credit card or a light bill to tell others about His greatness in our life. Then we can also invite those who open our envelope to get to know a little more about our Savior and Lord, Jesus Christ.

How might you two use similar opportunities to witness and share Christ's love with your creditors who always seem to remember you each month? Share His love and remember to pray for them as well.

EXCERPT 64

A Foreclosure?

We had rented a house in a subdivision in Florida. We called it "the mustard house" because the owners had painted the whole inside of the house mustard yellow. It was a challenge to decorate, but not wanting to do the repainting of twelve-foot-high ceilings, we decided to work with "mustard."

We settled into the house in July for what we thought would be at least till Buck's retirement three years later. Our three-bedroom home allowed for Buck's hobby room, my art room, and our huge master bedroom, along with a living room, kitchen, laundry room, garage, and two full baths. There was a creek out back where ducks, fish, and frogs entertained us. Sand hill cranes also wandered through the neighborhood, making their presence known by begging for food with their horrible squawks. In addition to this horrible sound announcing their presence, their pecking beaks liked to eat the bugs off the screen on our screened-in porch. That pecking literally poked holes and destroyed the screen as they feasted on their luxurious gourmet treats.

As we began to enjoy the neighborhood, met a few of the neighbors, enjoyed bike rides or walks at night, we considered purchasing this "mustard" house. However, that idea of purchase suddenly came to a halt one Saturday morning with a pounding knock at the front door.

Buck had left for work early on that Saturday morning. At 9 a.m., I heard a knock at the front door. Since I was not expecting company, I finished what I was doing and went to the front door an hour later. When I opened it, I found a bright yellow sheet of paper taped to the door with the word "Foreclosure" in capital letters at the top. When I telephoned the number on the paper, the gentleman who had served the notice explained this was a compliment of our court. As a tenant, we needed to know the landlord had not paid his mortgage for several months. He told me we were not legally responsible, but we would eventually have to move due to the bank's handling of the property. In checking with representatives of the mortgage company, the bank, etc., we found we had no choice but to look for another place to live.

The next few weeks were spent in prayer, asking the Lord to guide our steps as to where to begin to look and to provide what He felt we needed. We asked Him to lead us to the location of our next home. I looked in the papers and called several companies, real estate agents, etc. Finally I located a house in Merritt Island, twenty minutes from Buck's work, which would help so much since the price of gasoline at that time was approaching four dollars per gallon. The location would be perfect since Buck was working twelve- to fourteen-hour days. I set an appointment, went to look, and could not wait to show Buck. I called him at work to inform him of my find. We set an appointment to see the house that evening and together found a new place to reside. He especially enjoyed the three-car garage. I loved the large amount of storage and the view of the lake out back.

We worked to pack for the move with Buck loading the truck every night and leaving early every morning to unload at the new house before beginning his day of work at the Cape. This continued over a period of two weeks prior to the "big" move. We finally settled in what we both thought would be our final move before our scheduled retirement three years later.

God had other plans. His ways are not our ways. But, like our other stages of our life, we danced here in His love and in our romance. For that dance, I am eternally grateful.

Dance Tip 64

Residences are temporary. The manifold blessing of the Lord never ceases.

What kind of attitude adjustment is needed for us to get His proper perspective?

A Happy Homecoming, Mr. Sons!

My husband, Buck, was scheduled to arrive home at the Orlando airport at 9:45 p.m. from a ten-day business trip to California. That was the only part of the itinerary I knew. When he and I talked, I forgot to ask for flight information until we were off the phone. However, despite no flight number plus no terminal information, no name of his airline, nor even what originating city he was flying from (San Francisco or San Jose), I made a reservation at a motel near the airport for a surprise romantic rendezvous.

The adventure began when I arrived at the parking service we used when traveling. This service was the one that Buck *always* used when going out of town. I phoned them to see if Buck's truck was parked there. The lady looked for Buck's key packet quickly, but she had customers and suggested I call back in twenty minutes. I complied with her request. When I called back, she checked through the list twice. She said she had no name on the roster entry for Sons and no key packet. I explained to her that when we fly, we *never* use any other parking facility. She checked one more time and could find nothing under the name of Sons.

Oh well, I thought, *I'll just head to the airport anyway.* On the hour-and-a-half trip to the airport, I stopped at the office of the parking service. I explained I just wanted to surprise my husband. I asked for their permission to drive through their lot of parked cars to try to locate my husband's truck. Sure enough, it was there in the parking lot. I left Buck a note in the truck and proceeded back to the office to let them know what I'd found. They showed me the roster for that return date, and the third name from the top was my husband's name. I thanked them and asked if I could leave a note in his key packet. When they looked one more time, there was the key packet in his very own handwriting, and his truck keys were inside. I wrote another message on his key packet to call me on the cell phone when he got his keys. Off to the airport I went.

I parked my car, entered the airport like a lost puppy, and walked to the big information board in the terminal, trying to guess his airline and planned arrival by 9:45 p.m. (which was all I knew). Since he would be coming in from either San Francisco or San Jose, I had no clue where to begin. I did know he had a long layover in a city. I just didn't know which one. I then realized the information would not be listed by origination city. It would be listed by stopover city. Oh my!

How was I going to find his flight? I checked the information board on side A. Nothing looked promising, even though I didn't know what the definition of "promising" might look like. I walked to side B, but all I found was a large section of TV terminals with arrivals and departures. Since I didn't know the stopover city, I just decided to start watching all the people getting off the planes on side B starting at 9:45 p.m. That should work!

You guessed it! Nothing! I looked at the monitors one last time and headed back to side A to stare at the big board as they periodically updated changes to add new flight arrivals. I couldn't even guess his arrival flight from the information posted.

I prayed and realized I had done all I could do. I decided a decaf mocha might be in order. I sat down and tried to relax with my coffee and waited. At 11:30 p.m., there was nothing—no handsome husband and no cell phone call.

I made the decision rather than spending more money on airport parking, I'd head back to the parking service and wait for Buck there. He would have to show up there to pick up his truck. Though their waiting room was very sparse, it shouldn't have been too long. When I arrived at the parking facility and drove through the parking lot again, Buck's truck was *not there*! I had not received a phone call. I returned to the parking service office and asked if they had given my message to my husband. They said they had given him the message, and he'd left within the half hour. I was stunned. Where could he be?

As I returned to my van and opened the door, my cell phone was ringing. It was 11:45 p.m. *It was my honey!* He was a mile down the road at a pay phone. His cell phone battery was dead. He had arrived into side B at the airport on the tarmac, but there had been a lengthy delay in getting the passengers off the plane. Then there was an even longer delay of over an hour waiting to be picked up by our favorite and most efficient parking service.

We drove to the motel, checked in, and went out for a 12:30 a.m. "dinner" to share our exciting adventures. Dinner was great, and we later (or should I say "earlier"?) settled into a much-needed time of rest and recuperation.

Happy homecoming, Mr. Sons!

Dance Tip 65

While my intentions were grand, I could have improved on my attention to detail. But why would I want to do that? Adventures only come around once in life, and you must grab them on the run to keep the spice and spark interesting and exciting! My advice: never get so caught up in the details that you miss the joy of the unknown! Some people might call this irresponsible. Not me! That's one thing that put the "zazz" in our "pizzazz!"

Take the time to discuss how you two perhaps get so lost in the details that you miss the spontaneity that can be such a great adventure. So what if you're late? So what if you don't follow every detail to the letter? So what if you are inconvenienced by misinformation? So what?

Are you willing to dance in the middle of the adventure?

Art Works!

There was an exciting working artist art show coming up in Florida. Since I'd been doing portrait drawing using graphite pencils for just a year, I didn't enter the show.

However, one of the ladies on the show committee visited a gallery where my work was displayed. Looking at my work, she invited me to participate in this great show. Buck encouraged me to go for it. I had no tent, but a friend made hers available to me. I had no walls on which to hang my work nor any print bins, but a friend offered to let me borrow the ones she used for the shows.

So Buck and I packed my art, and we became participants in an art fair entitled, "ArtWorks 2007." I worked on a piece of artwork as people came by my booth to learn more about creating pencil portraits. We were encouraged by how well we were received and the interest they expressed. Of course, lots of friends came by to say "Hi" as well.

Buck remarked how much he enjoyed participating in the art show with me. He shared with me that when we attended other shows, we walked, looked at the art, etc., but we never got to spend any time with the artists. However as a participant, he got to spend quite a lot of time talking with the artists, visiting with them at their booths, learning about their lives, and finding out the techniques they used in creating their masterpieces.

Dance Tip 66

We danced, even through a silly thing like participating in an outdoor art show. We were partners in life on the greatest dance floor.

How are your dance steps coming along? Are they working together in smooth, syncopated rhythm, or are they a little out of step?

Do you need to go back to the footsteps on the floor and rehearse the 1-2-3-4 a few more times at this stage in life? A little spit and polish is always worth the reward!

EXCERPT 67

A "Buck" Letter to a Friend

I found a letter Buck had written to his friend with Lou Gehrig's disease. This man had to leave their place of employment and later died, leaving behind a wife and two children. His letter read as follows:

Dear John:

I thought you might enjoy my first impressions of you, engineering lead man. I didn't get to interface with you much until I began work on a particular product. I thought you were a neat guy, but someone sharp enough mentally to really be a formidable adversary—you know, somebody who could chew you up and spit you out while they hummed classical music under their breath. I noted that you particularly gave one of our team members a rough time and seemed to enjoy watching him squirm.

But I found a ministry poster prominently displayed in your cubicle an intriguing facet of who you were. I then had the privilege to find out about our project and the man who was there when it was born and who had nurtured and shaped it to full adulthood. What a pleasant surprise for you to openly share about the monster machine even though I was messing around with something you'd spent a sizeable chunk of your life perfecting! Thanks for answering all my silly little questions while I came to grips with how the thing worked.

Then I found out you were a kindred spirit when it came to a passionate interest in things that fly—not just missiles, but things with wings, rotors, and probably feathers, too.

I enjoyed my time with you and would like to point out that you're stuck with me for eternity, Dude. Thanks for keeping Lin and me abreast of the challenges you have been presented with in this disease. You know, man, when you moved on from our place of employment and you placed those books on the "free shelf" there in that old part of our world, it really struck me how you had prayerfully looked at all the facts you could amass about your challenge and made an immediate switch to doing what was most important—taking care of your wife and family in every concentrated fashion you could come up with, putting yourself last.

We all know we're only given one day at a time, but we (if you're anything like the rest of us) don't dwell on it much. We just muddle our way meandering down the trail of life. You're the trailblazer of our little depraved group of engineer types. Only the bravest are considered worthy enough to carry the flag into battle. We are in God's army, you see.

Our prayers are with you and for you and your family. Please think on and pray for us, my friend, and brother in Christ.

Dance Tip 67

Love, intense friendship, and respect in Christ are God's greatest gifts we humans are allowed to experience with other human beings. While I could write on and on about my husband, I think this sharing with his friend gives a glance inside my man's heart. He took the time to appreciate and share his respect with his friend. What a life lesson! The compassion of Christ is often found in human form. What an example!

Buck didn't "collect" friends. He cared for people and showered them with respect and attention. He lived Jesus' compassion out loud. I pray you know the difference between quoting Scripture, intellectually studying, etc., and really living the love of Christ to your friends and family.

How might you two make a few steps in your dance to intensify your "love language" to those you hold dear?

Estes Park—to and from 2009

The first time Buck and I went to Estes Park was one of wonder, excitement, anticipation, and an overwhelming sense of awe. We were attending ministry training on the campus of a nearby university. Our new assignment from the Lord and from the ministry (as we understood it) was to write the training manual for speaker couples, select and train those couples, and go out and minister God's Word throughout the country.

A retired man and his wife asked us to ride up to Estes Park one afternoon to discuss our assignment. On the way up the mountain, the man asked if we could do the job. We answered, "No, but through the Lord's guidance and strength, we would do the job." He let us know we were his choice, and he would get everything set up for our future move to Virginia.

God had always looked out for us as we gave Him our new adventure and held on as He ordered our steps. He provided Buck an engineering job there, and we set up a house-hunting trip to Virginia.

We looked and looked to find the just right apartment. When we found the right one, we entered our name on the list and gave them our anticipated move-in date that was based on Buck's start date. Once our application to the apartment complex was approved, we received a phone call that we were number twelve on the list for an apartment in that complex—*number twelve.*

Okay, so number twelve it was. We prayed and waited. As Buck's job date got closer and closer, we had received no phone call from the apartment management. Yes, we began to wonder what the Lord had in mind, but we trusted that His timing was perfect.

A week from his start date, we received a call saying that the apartment we wanted had become available. I questioned the caller how that could possibly have happened since we were number twelve. The caller explained all those on the list before us had been contacted. For credit reasons, change of job status, or a change in their desired location, everyone ahead of us had dropped off the list ahead of us. She asked, "When would you like to take possession?"

We prayed, thanked the Lord for His provision, contacted the movers, and were in place in our most desired apartment with Buck reporting for work the following week. I took my position for us at the ministry.

Lots of hurt and pain followed from events at the ministry. Buck and I were so certain in our hearts and spirits God had called us to that work. When man had been so cruel, I was devastated in my heart and spirit. I could forgive them, but I could not release the pain. Buck kept telling me to "let it go," and I knew what he was telling me was true. I absolutely could not find the freedom to forgive on my own.

After a year or so there, the Lord clearly brought to our mind to shake the dust off our feet and move on to another area. We did just that in the Lord's timing and His provision by returning to Florida. Later we made the switch in ministry.

However, eight years later, I knew I was to return to the Estes Park area for a pencil workshop to learn new skills in my portrait artwork. Often what we deem as obscure becomes obvious in God's eyes and direction. I had three days in Colorado between a portrait conference in DC and the pencil workshop in this mountain community. I did some driving to check out several cities, but knew I was just passing time. I kept asking God to speak to me. I just wanted and needed to hear from Him.

On the third day, I didn't have any plans. I just started driving and decided to drive up to Estes Park to the Rocky Mountain National Park. As I thought through that, the memory was very painful and I reminded the Lord. It was more because Buck and I had made this drive together, and now I was alone because of his death. I labored over the devastation of the ministry and my holding on to the misery and pain, now coupled with the grief in my loss of my husband just a few months before.

I drove to the park entrance, paid my fee, and, in tears, began the winding road to the top of one of the areas. I painfully relived all of the conversations with the man and his wife we'd had as we made this drive together. I replayed all the ministry's promises and reminded the Lord how Buck was the right man chosen by Him to lead the speaker team. I reminded him how all the participants in our seminars loved Buck because he was so gentle and relatable. I also cried and told the Lord I just couldn't hang on to all this pain anymore. I remembered Buck's many reminders once again to let it go. As I drove on, I had a monologue with God that went like this: "Okay, Lord, in this peace and quiet of the mountains, now talk to me. Can't you hear me *listening?*"

Somehow, about three-quarters of the way up the drive, in tears I realized I was now *free* of that devastation. I truly felt like a *big* load had been lifted from me. I had a new freedom because God had met me there on the road up that mountain and had freed me of those burdens in my heart. I felt such a peace as I stepped out of my car at the top of the mountain to view God's handiwork. Though I could see dark storm clouds approaching in the distance, there was sunshine where I was standing at the top of that mountain. I could praise Him in my heart with peace because of what He had done within me!

I am here to testify of His power, to glorify Him, and to give all the honor and praise to Him for always going before me and guiding my steps. While the pencil workshop was amazing, I know that the workshop was not the reason for my stay in Colorado. God had something bigger and more majestic in mind than the Rocky Mountains! He blessed me with new freedom because of His power!

Dance Tip 68

I had a choice. I could wallow or climb. I chose to climb. I had to fight through my emotions to experience the very best God had for me—His gift of freedom from past circumstances.

Couples often wallow in devastation when they need to experience the freedom Jesus gives. All it takes is release from the chains that bind us to those circumstances. Only He has the key. Jesus came to set the captives free!

In what circumstance are you choosing to live in the valley rather than allowing God to free you on the mountaintop?

EXCERPT 69

Myles—an Autobiography

In 2001, I wrote this tribute in honor of our green 1981 Honda. We were going to pass this tribute along as a very creative approach for much needed transportation for ministry. However, we decided it was a keepsake, and we never did send it to a Honda corporation. *Enjoy!* (Some of you men will be able to relate to our affection for Myles.)

My tribute read:

"In 1981, I, Myles, was a brand-new green Honda Civic Wagon. The Sons family, whose children were ten and six, adopted me. I became a vital part of their family and their missionary journey in serving the Lord by taking His Word to marriages around the USA. I've carried slide projectors, registration forms, written material, and all sorts of ministry supplies…and lots of luggage. I've also provided the son with dependable transportation to his first prom, watched as both children have left for college, and been a part of nine moves as my owner has been in the aerospace industry thirty years as of this writing. In fact, both children began their driving careers as I eagerly and patiently maneuvered with them through that process to celebrate success when they reached the age of ten.

I experienced a great deal of rejection from those children later as my beauty faded, and a new 1987 shiny white Honda took my place as the "family car." Because my body was rusted and I had such high mileage, I was nicknamed Myles. I was told I was a cousin to the British Porsche, the family's other dream car. My dependability served me well, and I gained great status in the eyes of this growing family. I continued on my missionary journey, crossing the country from one marriage ministry event to another, carrying this family back and forth in their moves across the USA.

My motto: -- Myles is my name; dependability is my game. --

The year is now 2001 and my body is shot. There are rust holes in the ceiling *and* in the floorboard. My engine is as strong as ever after over

181

311,000 miles. Both the children (who learned to drive with me) are grown now, and it's close to time for me to retire. I have been a part of their vital ministry of the Lord to marriages in Missouri, Florida, California, Texas, Arkansas, and now Virginia.

I can't think of a better vehicle to take over my job for this family than another Honda, the family choice. I'm no longer able to trek back and forth across the USA, but the need for dependable transportation is imperative. You see, my owners continue to serve as missionaries and need to travel extensively to take God's Word to a needy people."

Dance Tip 69

We had a car that was loved and valued by us. Silly? Perhaps! Once again, though, we could use a car story to share the need for the gospel to go out to the uttermost parts of the earth. The lesson here is that while I wrote a cute story about our trusty Myles, I did not submit it to the Honda corporate office.

How often do we think of stepping out but retreat when people need to hear about Jesus? They need to hear how He was born, how He gave up His life for them on the cross, how He rose from the grave to give them life, and that He's coming back soon!

We must not retreat. We must dance before Him in obedience and let Him order our next step.

EXCERPT 70

Applying God's Plan for Marriage: by Buck

"Applying God's plan for marriage will get you the immediate attention of Satan and all of his demons. It puts you and your spouse on the front lines of spiritual warfare. I can't emphasize enough the importance of daily putting on the full armor of God (Ephesians 6:10–18).

Okay ... how do we keep each article of armor in good shape? I'm really glad you asked. There are several things I've found that make a difference. We're to take things one day at a time—count the cost before you begin anything, but do so without listening to Satan's lies about your unworthiness. Ask God's forgiveness and then forgive yourself for what has transpired in the past. (That's why Christ went to the cross—to die for our sins. When we ask Him to be the Lord of our lives, He takes care of those. Asking daily is a good idea.)

Prayerfully look to the future and seek God's plan, but see that your main focus is today. Ask God daily for your needs and the needs of those around you. Develop the mind-set that when you are God's kid, anything over twenty-four hours is ancient history. Don't let the sun go down on your anger. Be angry and sin not. Resolve things. Don't keep a scorecard on yourself or your spouse. Easy? Not hardly, but doable if we look to the Holy Spirit for knowledge and wisdom in all things.

Jesus was a realist. He fully realized the fickleness of depraved human nature as well as the forces of Satan in this world against humanity. When daily temptation raises its ugly (sometimes beautiful) head, call upon Christ like so: audibly say, "In the name of Jesus Christ, get thee behind me, Satan. You have no power over a child of God. You know that, but so do I. Leave this place." Stand your ground.

Let your full armor do what it is designed to do—quench those fiery darts. Be sure you study and know what the Bible says. Satan knows and trembles, but he will challenge our understanding of what God said like he did with Eve in the Garden of Eden. Don't fall for that old trick. Call on the Holy Spirit for wisdom. Be the vessel that God can use for His purpose."

Dance Tip 70

Ephesians 6:10–18 defines the armor we need. Buck prayed that prayer over us daily, that we would be covered by the full armor of God and we would learn to accept and apply it to our life situations. God has thought of everything.

My challenge to you is to incorporate Ephesians 6:10–18 for a determined amount of time through prayer, study, and application. What a difference it made in our lives as warriors in the Kingdom!

How might it impact your life should you choose to take on this challenge?

Our Last Dance

Buck had worked twelve hours on Tuesday. Twelve- and fourteen-hour days six days a week had been the norm for a couple of years. He came home worn out.

We had dinner and had settled in for a quiet evening at home. He watched some TV. I cleaned up the kitchen after our meal, and we sat in our recliners to talk. We turned off the TV and just talked about the day's events and our agendas for the next few weeks. Then we got caught up to date about news from our phone conversations with Bruce and Heather.

All of a sudden, Buck stood up from his recliner. He held out his hand to me in invitation, and I stood up at such a welcomed time. Buck took me in his arms, and we danced together—to no music, just to the love we shared. He still chose me as his dance partner after almost forty years of marriage.

What a treasured memory as that dance turned out to be our last. Life presented us with his stroke the next morning and his death nine days later due to a pulmonary embolism.

No words left unspoken. The assurance and security of our love of each other was our gift to one another. In Buck's words, "No woulda, coulda, shoulda's."

No going back. No secrets. Complete!

We were very blessed to be able to dance in steps ordered by our Lord!

Dance Tip 71

From our years and years of sharing with married couples, we have seen there is so much unhappiness and intolerance in marriages today. Wounds have been inflicted, forgiveness has not been granted, walls have built up, dwellings house two individuals under the guise of marriage, but there often is no happiness and joy between the two.

Life is precious and your marriage can end quite abruptly. Let it end in love and joy with no words left unspoken, assurance and security of love for each other, no "woulda, coulda, shoulda's," no going back, no secrets—complete!

We are complete—not of our own accord or worthiness, but complete in Him (Colossians 2:10).

Our marriages are a witness, not to ourselves, but to the world around us of Christ's love. He is the Bridegroom and we are His Bride. Share His love first within your marriage to completeness. Then go out into the world, sharing your contagious love with all those you meet for His glory!

As I've shared throughout this book, Buck and I were not perfect. We were two "imperfects" who were joined together under the lordship of Jesus Christ to reflect His love to the world around us. We struggled and stumbled and stepped on each other's toes as we danced in our marriage relationship. Every couple does. But the best part was that we have the One who loves us so much He wants us to know His love, His joy, and His peace. All we had to do was to ask for Him to make us complete in Him.

I pray you will ask Him to be Lord of your marriage, that you ask Him to complete you, and that you two join Him in His dance. There is nothing sweeter than dancing in the joy of the Lord.

Are you two living in the love of Christ Jesus and in His joy? If tomorrow morning were your last, would you have a marriage defined as "no words unspoken, no "'woulda, coulda, shoulda's," no going back, no secrets—complete?"

My Testimony

Lin Sons

My story actually began before my birth. You see, due to various complications, my mom and dad waited thirteen years to welcome their first child. However, when my mother was close to delivery, the doctors warned her she would need to take a set of clothes for me to be buried in and a set of clothes to take me home from the hospital. Due to childhood rheumatic fever, my mother had suffered heart damage. The doctors did not expect mother or baby to make it through the delivery. We made it. God had other plans.

At five years old, I was asked to sing a solo in our children's program at church titled, "I'll Be a Sunbeam for Jesus." That became my life theme after hearing the story of my physical birth. I had a purpose and the gift of physical life. As I grew into my teen years, though my parents did not attend church at that time, as soon as I got my driver's license, I took my brother and attended church every Sunday. At sixteen, during a revival service at our church, God drew me to Himself through the Scripture found in Romans 5:5: "And hope maketh not ashamed; because the love of God is shed abroad in our hearts by the Holy Ghost which is given unto us." (KJV)

Soon after I accepted Christ, my earthly father died when he was run over after falling from a piece of road construction equipment upon which he was riding. He died ten hours later. I struggled with and questioned God about why He had taken my dad. I was angry and hurt and disappointed in my early walk in the Lord at that time. I didn't understand. Yet I knew deep down that He would take care of me if I walked as His child.

God says in Romans 8:28–29, "All things work together for good," and I knew these words had to apply to all situations, not just in the great times. God began to show me that He would never leave me nor forsake me (Joshua 1:9).

Just as God had given me physical life from the beginning, He would provide for me in the spiritual life through His Son, Jesus Christ, as my Savior first, and later as Lord of my life.

I live to serve—the very reason I am here today. God not only provided physical life when there was little or no chance for me to live. He also provided eternal life in the spiritual realm. He called me to Himself during that revival service, and I surrendered to His call. I live and love and serve Him today because He *is* the reason for my very existence.

Your Invitation to Dance before the Lord Jesus Christ

J ust as Buck issued me an invitation that first night we met, I issue you an invitation.

Perhaps there might be someone reading this who does not know Jesus Christ. You may have heard about Him, or maybe you want to know Him better. Seeking Him is quite simple. Just pray a prayer and ask Him to come into your life and tell Him you desire to follow Him as Savior and Lord—something like:

> Jesus, I know I need you. I know I am a sinner. I ask you to forgive me. I believe you died on that cross to save me. You rose from the grave to give us eternal life. You live today to be my Savior and Lord. Please come into my heart. In Jesus' name, Amen!

If you prayed that prayer, let me be the second to welcome you into the family of God! You see, Jesus is the first! Share your new decision with someone as the Lord prompts you. Go and tell … (Matthew 28:18–20).

If you have any questions or want to know how to learn more about your new decision, please contact me at *bucklin1@juno.com*. It will be my privilege to respond.

CPSIA information can be obtained at www.ICGtesting.com
Printed in the USA
BVOW02s1340070114

341074BV00004B/6/P